50 LANGUAGES

English (UK) – Ukrainian
for beginners

IMPRINT / IMPRESSUM

Johannes Schumann:
50LANGUAGES English (UK) - Ukrainian for beginners
EAN-13 (ISBN-13): 978-1-64018-164-9

Inquiries / Anfragen:
info@50languages.com
info@goethe-verlag.com

Table of contents

1 [one]

People

1 [один]
1 [odyn]

Особи
Osoby

I	Я YA
I and you	я і ти ya i ty
both of us	ми обидва / обидві my obydva / obydvi
he	Він Vin
he and she	він і вона vin i vona
they both	вони обидва / обидві vony obydva / obydvi
the man	Чоловік Cholovik
the woman	Жінка Zhinka
the child	Дитина Dytyna

1 [one]

1 [один]
1 [odyn]

People

Особи
Osoby

a family — сім’я
sim”ya

my family — моя сім’я
moya sim”ya

My family is here. — Моя сім’я тут.
Moya sim”ya tut.

I am here. — Я тут.
YA tut.

You are here. — Ти тут.
Ty tut.

He is here and she is here. — Він тут і вона тут.
Vin tut i vona tut.

We are here. — Ми тут.
My tut.

You are here. — Ви тут.
Vy tut.

They are all here. — Вони всі тут.
Vony vsi tut.

2 [two]

Family Members

2 [два]
2 [dva]

Сім'я
Sim"ya

the grandfather	Дідусь Didus'
the grandmother	Бабуся Babusya
he and she	він і вона vin i vona
the father	Батько Bat'ko
the mother	Мати Maty
he and she	він і вона vin i vona
the son	Син Syn
the daughter	Дочка Dochka
he and she	він і вона vin i vona

2 [two]

Family Members

2 [два]
2 [dva]

Сім’я
Sim”ya

the brother	Брат Brat
the sister	Сестра Sestra
he and she	він і вона vin i vona
the uncle	Дядько Dyad’ko
the aunt	Тітка Titka
he and she	він і вона vin i vona
We are a family.	Ми сім’я. My sim”ya.
The family is not small.	Сім’я не маленька. Sim”ya ne malen’ka.
The family is big.	Сім’я велика. Sim”ya velyka.

3 [three]

3 [три]
3 [try]

Getting to know others

Знайомство
Znaўomstvo

Hi!	Привіт! Pryvit!
Hello!	Доброго дня! Dobroho dnya!
How are you?	Як справи? Yak spravy?
Do you come from Europe?	Ви з Європи? Vy z Yevropy?
Do you come from America?	Ви з Америки? Vy z Ameryky?
Do you come from Asia?	Ви з Азії? Vy z Aziï?
In which hotel are you staying?	У якому готелі Ви проживаєте? U yakomu hoteli Vy prozhyvayete?
How long have you been here for?	Як довго Ви вже тут? Yak dovho Vy vzhe tut?
How long will you be staying?	Як надовго Ви залишаєтеся? Yak nadovho Vy zalyshayetesya?

3 [three]

3 [три]

3 [try]

Getting to know others

Знайомство

Znaŷomstvo

Do you like it here?

Чи подобається Вам тут?

Chy podobayet'sya Vam tut?

Are you here on vacation?

Ви тут у відпустці?

Vy tut u vidpusttsi?

Please do visit me sometime!

Відвідайте мене!

Vidvidaŷte mene!

Here is my address.

Ось моя адреса.

Os' moya adresa.

Shall we see each other tomorrow?

Ми побачимося завтра?

My pobachymosya zavtra?

I am sorry, but I already have plans.

На жаль, я вже щось запланував / запланувала.

Na zhal', ya vzhe shchos' zaplanuvav / zaplanuvala.

Bye!

Бувайте!

Buvaŷte!

Good bye!

До побачення!

Do pobachennya!

See you soon!

До зустрічі!

Do zustrichi!

4 [four]

4 [чотири]
4 [chotyry]

At school

В школі
V shkoli

Where are we?	Де ми? De my?
We are at school.	Ми в школі. My v shkoli.
We are having class / a lesson.	Ми маємо уроки. My mayemo uroky.
Those are the school children.	Це учні. Tse uchni.
That is the teacher.	Це вчителька. Tse vchytel'ka.
That is the class.	Це клас. Tse klas.
What are we doing?	Що ми робимо? Shcho my robymo?
We are learning.	Ми вчимося. My vchymosya.
We are learning a language.	Ми вивчаємо мову. My vyvchayemo movu.

4 [four]

4 [чотири]
4 [chotyry]

At school

В школі
V shkoli

I learn English.
Я вивчаю англійську мову.
YA vyvchayu anhliy̆s'ku movu.

You learn Spanish.
Ти вивчаєш іспанську мову.
Ty vyvchayesh ispans'ku movu.

He learns German.
Він вивчає німецьку мову.
Vin vyvchaye nimets'ku movu.

We learn French.
Ми вивчаємо французьку мову.
My vyvchayemo frantsuz'ku movu.

You all learn Italian.
Ви вивчаєте італійську мову.
Vy vyvchayete italiy̆s'ku movu.

They learn Russian.
Вони вивчають російську мову.
Vony vyvchayut' rosiy̆s'ku movu.

Learning languages is interesting.
Вивчати мови цікаво.
Vyvchaty movy tsikavo.

We want to understand people.
Ми хочемо розуміти людей.
My khochemo rozumity lyudey̆.

We want to speak with people.
Ми хочемо спілкуватися з людьми.
My khochemo spilkuvatysya z lyud'my.

5 [five]

Countries and Languages

5 [п’ять]
5 [p”yat’]

Країни і мови
Kraïny i movy

John is from London.	Джон з Лондону. Dzhon z Londonu.
London is in Great Britain.	Лондон розташований у Великобританії. London roztashovanyǔ u Velykobrytaniï.
He speaks English.	Він .розмовляє англійською. Vin .rozmovlyaye anhliǔs’koyu.
Maria is from Madrid.	Марія з Мадрида. Mariya z Madryda.
Madrid is in Spain.	Мадрид розташований в Іспанії. Madryd roztashovanyǔ v Ispaniï.
She speaks Spanish.	Вона розмовляє іспанською. Vona rozmovlyaye ispans’koyu.
Peter and Martha are from Berlin.	Петро і Марта – з Берліна. Petro i Marta – z Berlina.
Berlin is in Germany.	Берлін розташований у Німеччині. Berlin roztashovanyǔ u Nimechchyni.
Do both of you speak German?	Чи розмовляєте ви обидва німецькою? Chy rozmovlyayete vy obydva nimets’koyu?

5 [five]

5 [п'ять]
5 [p"yat']

Countries and Languages

Країни і мови
Kraïny i movy

London is a capital city.

Лондон – це столиця.
London – tse stolytsya.

Madrid and Berlin are also capital cities.

Мадрид та Берлін – це також столиці.
Madryd ta Berlin – tse takozh stolytsi.

Capital cities are big and noisy.

Столиці – великі і галасливі.
Stolytsi – velyki i halaslyvi.

France is in Europe.

Франція розташована в Європі.
Frantsiya roztashovana v Yevropi.

Egypt is in Africa.

Єгипет розташований в Африці.
Yehypet roztashovanyў v Afrytsi.

Japan is in Asia.

Японія розташована в Азії.
Yaponiya roztashovana v Aziï.

Canada is in North America.

Канада розташована в Північній Америці.
Kanada roztashovana v Pivnichniў Amerytsi.

Panama is in Central America.

Панама розташована у Центральній Америці .
Panama roztashovana u Tsentral'niў Amerytsi .

Brazil is in South America.

Бразилія розташована в Південній Америці.
Brazyliya roztashovana v Pivdenniў Amerytsi.

6 [six]

Reading and writing

6 [шість]
6 [shist']

Читати і писати
Chytaty i pysaty

I read.

I read a letter.

I read a word.

I read a sentence.

I read a letter.

I read a book.

I read.

You read.

He reads.

Я читаю.
YA chytayu.
Я читаю літеру.
YA chytayu literu.
Я читаю слово.
YA chytayu slovo.

Я читаю речення.
YA chytayu rechennya.
Я читаю лист.
YA chytayu lyst.
Я читаю книгу.
YA chytayu knyhu.

Я читаю.
YA chytayu.
Ти читаєш.
Ty chytayesh.
Він читає.
Vin chytaye.

6 [six]

Reading and writing

6 [шість]
6 [shist']

Читати і писати
Chytaty i pysaty

I write.	Я пишу. YA pyshu.
I write a letter / character.	Я пишу літеру. YA pyshu literu.
I write a word.	Я пишу слово. YA pyshu slovo.
I write a sentence.	Я пишу речення. YA pyshu rechennya.
I write a letter.	Я пишу лист. YA pyshu lyst.
I write a book.	Я пишу книгу. YA pyshu knyhu.
I write.	Я пишу. YA pyshu.
You write.	Ти пишеш. Ty pyshesh.
He writes.	Він пише. Vin pyshe.

7 [seven]

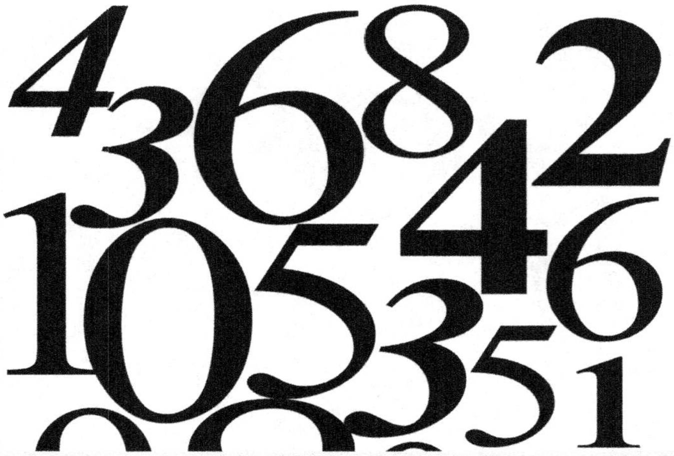

7 [сім]
7 [sim]

Numbers

Числа
Chysla

I count:

one, two, three

I count to three.

Я рахую:
YA rakhuyu:
один, два, три
odyn, dva, try
Я рахую до трьох.
YA rakhuyu do tr'okh.

I count further:

four, five, six,

seven, eight, nine

Я рахую далі:
YA rakhuyu dali:
Чотири, п'ять, шість,
Chotyry, p"yat', shist',
сім, вісім, дев'ять
sim, visim, dev"yat'

I count.

You count.

He counts.

Я рахую.
YA rakhuyu.
Ти рахуєш.
Ty rakhuyesh.
Він рахує.
Vin rakhuye.

7 [seven]

7 [сім]
7 [sim]

Numbers

Числа
Chysla

One. The first.
Two. The second.
Three. The third.

Один. Перший.
Odyn. Pershyў.
Два. Другий.
Dva. Druhyў.
Три. Третій.
Try. Tretiў.

Four. The fourth.
Five. The fifth.
Six. The sixth.

Чотири. Четвертий.
Chotyry. Chetvertyў.
П’ять. П’ятий.
P”yat’. P”yatyў.
Шість. Шостий.
Shist’. Shostyў.

Seven. The seventh.
Eight. The eighth.
Nine. The ninth.

Сім. Сьомий.
Sim. S’omyў.
Вісім. Восьмий.
Visim. Vos’myў.
Дев’ять. Дев’ятий.
Dev”yat’. Dev”yatyў.

8 [eight]

The time

8 [вісім]
8 [visim]

Години доби

Hodyny doby

Excuse me!
Вибачте!
Vybachte!

What time is it, please?
Скажіть будь-ласка, котра година?
Skazhit' bud'-laska, kotra hodyna?

Thank you very much.
Щиро дякую.
Shchyro dyakuyu.

It is one o'clock.
Перша година.
Persha hodyna.

It is two o'clock.
Друга година.
Druha hodyna.

It is three o'clock.
Третя година.
Tretya hodyna.

It is four o'clock.
Четверта година.
Chetverta hodyna.

It is five o'clock.
П'ята година.
P"yata hodyna.

It is six o'clock.
Шоста година.
Shosta hodyna.

8 [eight]

The time

8 [вісім]
8 [visim]

Години доби
Hodyny doby

It is seven o'clock.	Сьома година. S'oma hodyna.
It is eight o'clock.	Восьма година. Vos'ma hodyna.
It is nine o'clock.	Дев'ята година. Dev"yata hodyna.
It is ten o'clock.	Десята година. Desyata hodyna.
It is eleven o'clock.	Одинадцята година. Odynadtsyata hodyna.
It is twelve o'clock.	Дванадцята година. Dvanadtsyata hodyna.
A minute has sixty seconds.	Хвилина має шістдесят секунд. Khvylyna maye shistdesyat sekund.
An hour has sixty minutes.	Година має шістдесят хвилин. Hodyna maye shistdesyat khvylyn.
A day has twenty-four hours.	День має двадцять чотири години. Den' maye dvadtsyat' chotyry hodyny.

9 [nine]

9 [дев’ять]
9 [dev”yat’]

Days of the week

Дні тижня
Dni tyzhnya

Monday	Понеділок Ponedilok
Tuesday	Вівторок Vivtorok
Wednesday	Середа Sereda
Thursday	Четвер Chetver
Friday	п’ятниця p”yatnytsya
Saturday	Субота Subota
Sunday	Неділя Nedilya
the week	Тиждень Tyzhden’
from Monday to Sunday	від понеділка до неділі vid ponedilka do nedili

9 [nine]

9 [дев’ять]
9 [dev”yat’]

Days of the week

Дні тижня
Dni tyzhnya

The first day is Monday.	Перший день – понеділок. Pershyў den’ – ponedilok.
The second day is Tuesday.	Другий день – вівторок. Druhyў den’ – vivtorok.
The third day is Wednesday.	Третій день – середа. Tretiў den’ – sereda.
The fourth day is Thursday.	Четвертий день – четвер. Chetvertyў den’ – chetver.
The fifth day is Friday.	П’ятий день – п’ятниця. P”yatyў den’ – p”yatnytsya.
The sixth day is Saturday.	Шостий день – субота. Shostyў den’ – subota.
The seventh day is Sunday.	Сьомий день – неділя. S’omyў den’ – nedilya.
The week has seven days.	Тиждень має сім днів. Tyzhden’ maye sim dniv.
We only work for five days.	Ми працюємо лише п’ять днів. My pratsyuyemo lyshe p'yat’ dniv.

10 [ten]

Yesterday – today – tomorrow

10 [десять]
10 [desyat']

Вчора – сьогодні – завтра
Vchora – s'ohodni – zavtra

Yesterday was Saturday.	Вчора була субота. Vchora bula subota.
I was at the cinema yesterday.	Вчора я був / була у кіно. Vchora ya buv / bula u kino.
The film was interesting.	Фільм був цікавий. Fil'm buv tsikavyў.
Today is Sunday.	Сьогодні неділя. S'ohodni nedilya.
I'm not working today.	Сьогодні я не працюю. S'ohodni ya ne pratsyuyu.
I'm staying at home.	Я залишаюся вдома. YA zalyshayusya vdoma.
Tomorrow is Monday.	Завтра понеділок. Zavtra ponedilok.
Tomorrow I will work again.	Завтра я знову працюю. Zavtra ya znovu pratsyuyu.
I work at an office.	Я працюю в офісі. YA pratsyuyu v ofisi.

10 [ten]

Yesterday – today – tomorrow

10 [десять]
10 [desyat']

Вчора – сьогодні – завтра

Vchora – s'ohodni – zavtra

Who is that?	Хто це? Khto tse?
That is Peter.	Це Петро. Tse Petro.
Peter is a student.	Петро – студент. Petro – student.
Who is that?	Хто це? Khto tse?
That is Martha.	Це Марта. Tse Marta.
Martha is a secretary.	Марта – секретарка. Marta – sekretarka.
Peter and Martha are friends.	Петро і Марта – друзі. Petro i Marta – druzi.
Peter is Martha's friend.	Петро є другом Марти. Petro ye druhom Marty.
Martha is Peter's friend.	Марта є подругою Петра. Marta ye podruhoyu Petra.

11 [eleven]

Months

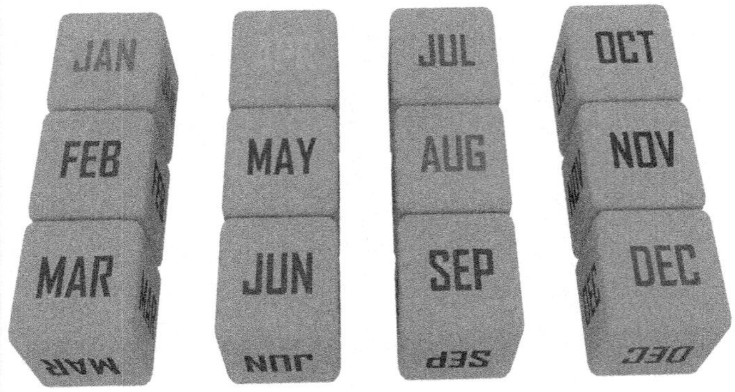

11 [одинадцять]
11 [odynadtsyat’]

Місяці
Misyatsi

January	Січень Sichen’
February	Лютий Lyutyў
March	Березень Berezen’
April	Квітень Kviten’
May	Травень Traven’
June	Червень Cherven’
These are six months.	Це шість місяців. Tse shist’ misyatsiv.
January, February, March,	Січень, лютий, березень, Sichen’, lyutyў, berezen’,
April, May and June.	квітень, травень і червень. kviten’, traven’ i cherven’.

11 [eleven] — 11 [одинадцять]
11 [odynadtsyat’]

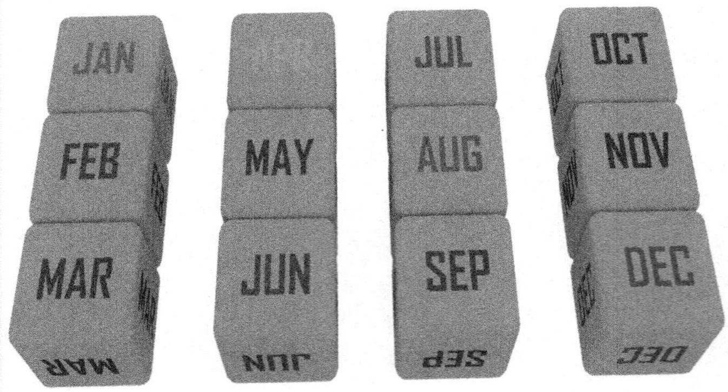

Months — Місяці
Misyatsi

July	Липень Lypen’
August	Серпень Serpen’
September	Вересень Veresen’
October	Жовтень Zhovten’
November	Листопад Lystopad
December	Грудень Hruden’
These are also six months.	Це також шість місяців. Tse takozh shist’ misyatsiv.
July, August, September,	Липень, серпень, вересень, Lypen’, serpen’, veresen’,
October, November and December.	жовтень, листопад і грудень. zhovten’, lystopad i hruden’.

12 [twelve]

12 [дванадцять]
12 [dvanadtsyat']

Beverages

Напої
Napoï

I drink tea.
Я п'ю чай.
YA p"yu chaў.

I drink coffee.
Я п'ю каву.
YA p"yu kavu.

I drink mineral water.
Я п'ю мінеральну воду.
YA p"yu mineral'nu vodu.

Do you drink tea with lemon?
Чи п'єш ти чай з лимоном?
Chy p"yesh ty chaў z lymonom?

Do you drink coffee with sugar?
Чи п'єш ти каву з цукром?
Chy p"yesh ty kavu z tsukrom?

Do you drink water with ice?
Чи п'єш ти воду з льодом?
Chy p"yesh ty vodu z l'odom?

There is a party here.
Тут вечірка.
Tut vechirka.

People are drinking champagne.
Люди п'ють шампанське.
Lyudy p"yut' shampans'ke.

People are drinking wine and beer.
Люди п'ють вино і пиво.
Lyudy p"yut' vyno i pyvo.

12 [twelve]

12 [дванадцять]
12 [dvanadtsyat']

Beverages

Напої
Napoï

Do you drink alcohol?
Чи п'єш ти алкоголь?
Chy p"yesh ty alkohol'?

Do you drink whisky / whiskey (am.)?
Чи п'єш ти віскі?
Chy p"yesh ty viski?

Do you drink Coke with rum?
Чи п'єш ти колу з ромом?
Chy p"yesh ty kolu z romom?

I do not like champagne.
Я не люблю шампанського.
YA ne lyublyu shampans'koho.

I do not like wine.
Я не люблю вина.
YA ne lyublyu vyna.

I do not like beer.
Я не люблю пива.
YA ne lyublyu pyva.

The baby likes milk.
Немовля любить молоко.
Nemovlya lyubyt' moloko.

The child likes cocoa and apple juice.
Дитина любить какао і яблучний сік.
Dytyna lyubyt' kakao i yabluchnyў sik.

The woman likes orange and grapefruit juice.
Жінка любить помаранчевий сік і грейпфрутовий сік.
Zhinka lyubyt' pomaranchevyў sik i hreўpfrutovyў sik.

13 [thirteen]

13 [тринадцять]
13 [trynadtsyat’]

Activities

Види діяльності
Vydy diyal’nosti

What does Martha do?	Що робить Марта? Shcho robyt’ Marta?
She works at an office.	Вона працює в офісі. Vona pratsyuye v ofisi.
She works on the computer.	Вона працює за комп’ютером. Vona pratsyuye za komp'yuterom.
Where is Martha?	Де Марта? De Marta?
At the cinema.	У кіно. U kino.
She is watching a film.	Вона дивиться фільм. Vona dyvyt’sya fil’m.
What does Peter do?	Що робить Петро? Shcho robyt’ Petro?
He studies at the university.	Він навчається в університеті. Vin navchayet’sya v universyteti.
He studies languages.	Він вивчає мови. Vin vyvchaye movy.

13 [thirteen]

13 [тринадцять]
13 [trynadtsyat’]

Activities

Види діяльності
Vydy diyal’nosti

Where is Peter?	Де Петро? De Petro?
At the café.	У кафе. U kafe.
He is drinking coffee.	Він п’є каву. Vin p”ye kavu.
Where do they like to go?	Куди вони люблять ходити? Kudy vony lyublyat’ khodyty?
To a concert.	На концерти. Na kontserty.
They like to listen to music.	Вони люблять слухати музику. Vony lyublyat’ slukhaty muzyku.
Where do they not like to go?	Куди вони не люблять ходити? Kudy vony ne lyublyat’ khodyty?
To the disco.	На дискотеку. Na dyskoteku.
They do not like to dance.	Вони не люблять танцювати. Vony ne lyublyat’ tantsyuvaty.

14 [fourteen]

14 [чотирнадцять]
14 [chotyrnadtsyat’]

Colors

Кольори
Kol’ory

Snow is white.	Сніг білий. Snih bilyў.
The sun is yellow.	Сонце жовте. Sontse zhovte.
The orange is orange.	Помаранча оранжева. Pomarancha oranzheva.
The cherry is red.	Вишня червона. Vyshnya chervona.
The sky is blue.	Небо синє. Nebo synye.
The grass is green.	Трава зелена. Trava zelena.
The earth is brown.	Земля коричнева. Zemlya korychneva.
The cloud is grey / gray (am.).	Хмара сіра. Khmara sira.
The tyres / tires (am.) are black.	Шини чорні. Shyny chorni.

14 [fourteen]

14 [чотирнадцять]
14 [chotyrnadtsyat’]

Colors

Кольори
Kol’ory

What colour / color (am.) is the snow? White.	Якого кольору сніг? Білий. Yakoho kol’oru snih? Bilyў.
What colour / color (am.) is the sun? Yellow.	Якого кольору сонце? Жовте. Yakoho kol’oru sontse? Zhovte.
What colour / color (am.) is the orange? Orange.	Якого кольору помаранча? Оранжева. Yakoho kol’oru pomarancha? Oranzheva.
What colour / color (am.) is the cherry? Red.	Якого кольору вишня? Червона. Yakoho kol’oru vyshnya? Chervona.
What colour / color (am.) is the sky? Blue.	Якого кольору небо? Синє. Yakoho kol’oru nebo? Synye.
What colour / color (am.) is the grass? Green.	Якого кольору трава? Зелена. Yakoho kol’oru trava? Zelena.
What colour / color (am.) is the earth? Brown.	Якого кольору земля? Коричнева. Yakoho kol’oru zemlya? Korychneva.
What colour / color (am.) is the cloud? Grey / Gray (am.).	Якого кольору хмара? Сіра. Yakoho kol’oru khmara? Sira.
What colour / color (am.) are the tyres / tires (am.)? Black.	Якого кольору шини? Чорні. Yakoho kol’oru shyny? Chorni.

15 [fifteen]

Fruits and food

15 [п'ятнадцять]
15 [p"yatnadtsyat']

Плоди та продукти харчування

Plody ta produkty kharchuvannya

I have a strawberry.	Я маю полуницю. YA mayu polunytsyu.
I have a kiwi and a melon.	Я маю ківі і диню. YA mayu kivi i dynyu.
I have an orange and a grapefruit.	Я маю помаранчу і грейпфрут. YA mayu pomaranchu i hreÿpfrut.
I have an apple and a mango.	Я маю яблуко і манго. YA mayu yabluko i manho.
I have a banana and a pineapple.	Я маю банан і ананас. YA mayu banan i ananas.
I am making a fruit salad.	Я роблю салат із фруктів. YA roblyu salat iz fruktiv.
I am eating toast.	Я їм грінку. YA ïm hrinku.
I am eating toast with butter.	Я їм грінку з маслом. YA ïm hrinku z maslom.
I am eating toast with butter and jam.	Я їм грінку з маслом і джемом. YA ïm hrinku z maslom i dzhemom.

15 [fifteen]

Fruits and food

15 [п'ятнадцять]
15 [p"yatnadtsyat']

Плоди та продукти харчування
Plody ta produkty kharchuvannya

I am eating a sandwich.

Я їм сандвіч.
YA ïm sandvich.

I am eating a sandwich with margarine.

Я їм сендвіч з маргарином.
YA ïm sendvich z marharynom.

I am eating a sandwich with margarine and tomatoes.

Я їм сендвіч з маргарином і помідором.
YA ïm sendvich z marharynom i pomidorom.

We need bread and rice.

Нам потрібні хліб і рис.
Nam potribni khlib i rys.

We need fish and steaks.

Нам потрібні риба і біфштекс.
Nam potribni ryba i bifshteks.

We need pizza and spaghetti.

Нам потрібні піца і спагеті.
Nam potribni pitsa i spaheti.

What else do we need?

Що нам ще потрібно?
Shcho nam shche potribno?

We need carrots and tomatoes for the soup.

Нам потрібна і морква і помідори для супу.
Nam potribna i morkva i pomidory dlya supu.

Where is the supermarket?

Де є супермаркет?
De ye supermarket?

16 [sixteen]

Seasons and Weather

16 [шістнадцять]
16 [shistnadtsyat’]

Пори року і погода
Pory roku i pohoda

These are the seasons: | Це пори року:
Tse pory roku:

Spring, summer, | Весна, літо.
Vesna, lito.

autumn / fall (am.) and winter. | Осінь і зима.
Osin’ i zyma.

The summer is warm. | Літо гаряче.
Lito haryache.

The sun shines in summer. | Влітку світить сонце.
Vlitku svityt’ sontse.

We like to go for a walk in summer. | Влітку ми охоче гуляємо.
Vlitku my okhoche hulyayemo.

The winter is cold. | Зима холодна.
Zyma kholodna.

It snows or rains in winter. | Взимку падає сніг або йде дощ.
Vzymku padaye snih abo ўde doshch.

We like to stay home in winter. | Взимку ми охоче залишаємося вдома.
Vzymku my okhoche zalyshayemosya vdoma.

16 [sixteen]

Seasons and Weather

16 [шістнадцять]
16 [shistnadtsyat']

Пори року і погода

Pory roku i pohoda

It is cold.
Холодно.
Kholodno.

It is raining.
Падає дощ.
Padaye doshch.

It is windy.
Вітряно.
Vitryano.

It is warm.
Тепло.
Teplo.

It is sunny.
Сонячно.
Sonyachno.

It is pleasant.
Ясно.
Yasno.

What is the weather like today?
Яка сьогодні погода?
Yaka s'ohodni pohoda?

It is cold today.
Сьогодні холодно.
S'ohodni kholodno.

It is warm today.
Сьогодні тепло.
S'ohodni teplo.

17 [seventeen]

17 [сімнадцять]
17 [simnadtsyat']

Around the house

У будинку
U budynku

Our house is here. | Це наш будинок.
TSe nash budynok.

The roof is on top. | Нагорі є дах.
Nahori ye dakh.

The basement is below. | Внизу є підвал.
Vnyzu ye pidval.

There is a garden behind the house. | За будинком є сад.
Za budynkom ye sad.

There is no street in front of the house. | Перед будинком немає вулиці.
Pered budynkom nemaye vulytsi.

There are trees next to the house. | Біля будинку є дерева.
Bilya budynku ye dereva.

My apartment is here. | Це моя квартира
TSe moya kvartyra

The kitchen and bathroom are here. | Тут є кухня і ванна кімната.
Tut ye kukhnya i vanna kimnata.

The living room and bedroom are there. | Там є вітальня і спальня.
Tam ye vital'nya i spal'nya.

17 [seventeen]

Around the house

17 [сімнадцять]
17 [simnadtsyat']

У будинку
U budynku

The front door is closed.

Вхідні двері зачинені.
Vkhidni dveri zachyneni.

But the windows are open.

Але вікна відчинені
Ale vikna vidchyneni

It is hot today.

Сьогодні спекотно.
S'ohodni spekotno.

We are going to the living room.

Ми йдемо у вітальню.
My ўdemo u vital'nyu.

There is a sofa and an armchair there.

Там є диван і крісло.
Tam ye dyvan i krislo.

Please, sit down!

Сідайте!
Sidaўte!

My computer is there.

Там стоїть мій комп'ютер.
Tam stoït' miў komp"yuter.

My stereo is there.

Там стоїть мій музичний центр.
Tam stoït' miў muzychnyў tsentr.

The TV set is brand new.

Телевізор зовсім новий.
Televizor zovsim novyў.

18 [eighteen]

House cleaning

18 [вісімнадцять]
18 [visimnadtsyat']

Прибирання в домі
Prybyrannya v domi

Today is Saturday.	Сьогодні субота. S'ohodni subota.
We have time today.	Сьогодні ми маємо час. S'ohodni my mayemo chas.
We are cleaning the apartment today.	Сьогодні ми прибираємо квартиру. S'ohodni my prybyrayemo kvartyru.
I am cleaning the bathroom.	Я прибираю ванну кімнату. YA prybyrayu vannu kimnatu.
My husband is washing the car.	Мій чоловік миє автомобіль. Miӳ cholovik myye avtomobil'.
The children are cleaning the bicycles.	Діти чистять велосипеди. Dity chystyat' velosypedy.
Grandma is watering the flowers.	Бабуся поливає квіти. Babusya polyvaye kvity.
The children are cleaning up the children's room.	Діти прибирають дитячу кімнату. Dity prybyrayut' dytyachu kimnatu.
My husband is tidying up his desk.	Мій чоловік прибирає свій письмовий стіл. Miӳ cholovik prybyraye sviӳ pys'movyӳ stil.

18 [eighteen]

House cleaning

18 [вісімнадцять]
18 [visimnadtsyat’]

Прибирання в домі
Prybyrannya v domi

I am putting the laundry in the washing machine.	Я кладу білизну в пральну машину. YA kladu bilyznu v pral’nu mashynu.
I am hanging up the laundry.	Я вішаю білизну. YA vishayu bilyznu.
I am ironing the clothes.	Я прасую білизну. YA prasuyu bilyznu.
The windows are dirty.	Вікна брудні. Vikna brudni.
The floor is dirty.	Підлога брудна. Pidloha brudna.
The dishes are dirty.	Посуд брудний. Posud brudnyў.
Who washes the windows?	Хто миє вікна? Khto myye vikna?
Who does the vacuuming?	Хто пилососить? Khto pylososyt’?
Who does the dishes?	Хто миє посуд? Khto myye posud?

19 [nineteen]

19 [дев’ятнадцять]
19 [dev”yatnadtsyat’]

In the kitchen

На кухні
Na kukhni

Do you have a new kitchen?

Ти маєш нову кухню?
Ty mayesh novu kukhnyu?

What do you want to cook today?

Що ти хочеш варити сьогодні?
Shcho ty khochesh varyty s’ohodni?

Do you cook on an electric or a gas stove?

Ти вариш на електриці чи на газі?
Ty varysh na elektrytsi chy na hazi?

Shall I cut the onions?

Чи повинен / повинна я різати цибулю?
Chy povynen / povynna ya rizaty tsybulyu?

Shall I peel the potatoes?

Чи повинен / повинна я чистити картоплю?
Chy povynen / povynna ya chystyty kartoplyu?

Shall I rinse the lettuce?

Чи повинен / повинна я мити салат?
Chy povynen / povynna ya myty salat?

Where are the glasses?

Де склянки?
De sklyanky?

Where are the dishes?

Де посуд?
De posud?

Where is the cutlery / silverware (am.)?

Де столові прибори?
De stolovi prybory?

19 [nineteen]

19 [дев'ятнадцять]
19 [dev"yatnadtsyat']

In the kitchen

На кухні
Na kukhni

Do you have a tin opener / can opener (am.)?	Чи маєш ти відкривач для консерв? Chy mayesh ty vidkryvach dlya konserv?
Do you have a bottle opener?	Чи маєш ти ключ для відкривання пляшок? Chy mayesh ty klyuch dlya vidkryvannya plyashok?
Do you have a corkscrew?	Чи маєш ти штопор? Chy mayesh ty shtopor?
Are you cooking the soup in this pot?	Чи вариш ти суп в цій каструлі? Chy varysh ty sup v tsiй kastruli?
Are you frying the fish in this pan?	Чи смажиш ти рибу на цій сковороді? Chy smazhysh ty rybu na tsiй skovorodi?
Are you grilling the vegetables on this grill?	Чи підсмажуєш ти овочі на решітці? Chy pidsmazhuyesh ty ovochi na reshittsi?
I am setting the table.	Я накриваю стіл. YA nakryvayu stil.
Here are the knives, the forks and the spoons.	Ось ножі, виделки і ложки. Os' nozhi, vydelky i lozhky.
Here are the glasses, the plates and the napkins.	Ось склянки, тарілки і серветки. Os' sklyanky, tarilky i servetky.

20 [twenty]

Small Talk 1

20 [двадцять]
20 [dvadtsyat']

Коротка розмова 1
Korotka rozmova 1

Make yourself comfortable!
Влаштовуйтесь зручніше!
Vlashtovuytes' zruchnishe!

Please, feel right at home!
Почувайтеся як удома!
Pochuvaytesya yak udoma!

What would you like to drink?
Що би Ви хотіли випити?
Shcho by Vy khotily vypyty?

Do you like music?
Ви любите музику?
Vy lyubyte muzyku?

I like classical music.
Я люблю класичну музику.
YA lyublyu klasychnu muzyku.

These are my CD's.
Тут є мої компакт-диски.
Tut ye moï kompakt-dysky.

Do you play a musical instrument?
Чи граєте Ви на якомусь інструменті?
Chy hrayete Vy na yakomus' instrumenti?

This is my guitar.
Ось моя гітара.
Os' moya hitara.

Do you like to sing?
Ви охоче співаєте?
Vy okhoche spivayete?

20 [twenty]

Small Talk 1

20 [двадцять]
20 [dvadtsyat']

Коротка розмова 1
Korotka rozmova 1

Do you have children?	Ви маєте дітей? Vy mayete diteў?
Do you have a dog?	Ви маєте собаку? Vy mayete sobaku?
Do you have a cat?	Ви маєте кішку? Vy mayete kishku?
These are my books.	Ось мої книги. Os' moï knyhy.
I am currently reading this book.	Я якраз читаю цю книгу. YA yakraz chytayu tsyu knyhu.
What do you like to read?	Що Ви охоче читаєте? Shcho Vy okhoche chytayete?
Do you like to go to concerts?	Чи Ви охоче ходите на концерти? Chy Vy okhoche khodyte na kontserty?
Do you like to go to the theatre / theater (am.)?	Чи Ви охоче ходите в театр? Chy Vy okhoche khodyte v teatr?
Do you like to go to the opera?	Чи Ви охоче ходите в оперний театр? Chy Vy okhoche khodyte v opernyў teatr?

21 [twenty-one]

21 [двадцять один]
21 [dvadtsyat' odyn]

Small Talk 2

Коротка розмова 2
Korotka rozmova 2

Where do you come from?
Звідки Ви?
Zvidky Vy?

From Basel.
З Базелю.
Z Bazelyu.

Basel is in Switzerland.
Базель розташований у Швейцарії.
Bazel' roztashovanyў u Shveўtsariï.

May I introduce Mr. Miller?
Дозвольте відрекомендувати Вам пана Мюллера.
Dozvol'te vidrekomenduvaty Vam pana Myullera.

He is a foreigner.
Він – іноземець.
Vin – inozemets'.

He speaks several languages.
Він розмовляє кількома мовами.
Vin rozmovlyaye kil'koma movamy.

Are you here for the first time?
Чи Ви вперше тут?
Chy Vy vpershe tut?

No, I was here once last year.
Ні, я був / була тут минулого року.
Ni, ya buv / bula tut mynuloho roku.

Only for a week, though.
Але тільки тиждень.
Ale til'ky tyzhden'.

21 [twenty-one]

Small Talk 2

21 [двадцять один]
21 [dvadtsyat' odyn]

Коротка розмова 2
Korotka rozmova 2

How do you like it here?
Чи подобається вам у нас?
Chy podobayet'sya vam u nas?

A lot. The people are nice.
Дуже добре. Люди приємні.
Duzhe dobre. Lyudy pryyemni.

And I like the scenery, too.
І місцевість подобається мені також.
I mistsevist' podobayet'sya meni takozh.

What is your profession?
Хто Ви за професією?
Khto Vy za profesiyeyu?

I am a translator.
Я перекладач.
YA perekladach.

I translate books.
Я перекладаю книги.
YA perekladayu knyhy.

Are you alone here?
Ви тут самі?
Vy tut sami?

No, my wife / my husband is also here.
Ні, моя жінка / мій чоловік також тут.
Ni, moya zhinka / miÿ cholovik takozh tut.

And those are my two children.
Там також двоє моїх дітей.
Tam takozh dvoye moïkh diteÿ.

22 [twenty-two]

Small Talk 3

22 [двадцять два]
22 [dvadtsyat' dva]

Коротка розмова 3

Korotka rozmova 3

Do you smoke?	Ви палите? Vy palyte?
I used to.	Раніше так. Ranishe tak.
But I don't smoke anymore.	Але тепер я більше не палю. Ale teper ya bil'she ne palyu.
Does it disturb you if I smoke?	Чи заважає Вам, коли я палю? Chy zavazhaye Vam, koly ya palyu?
No, absolutely not.	Ні, зовсім ні. Ni, zovsim ni.
It doesn't disturb me.	Це мені не заважає. Tse meni ne zavazhaye.
Will you drink something?	Ви щось п'єте? Vy shchos' p"yete?
A brandy?	Коньяк? Kon'yak?
No, preferably a beer.	Ні, краще пиво. Ni, krashche pyvo.

22 [twenty-two]

Small Talk 3

22 [двадцять два]
22 [dvadtsyat' dva]

Коротка розмова 3

Korotka rozmova 3

Do you travel a lot?	Ви багато подорожуєте? Vy bahato podorozhuyete?
Yes, mostly on business trips.	Так, переважно це ділові поїздки. Tak, perevazhno tse dilovi poïzdky.
But now we're on holiday.	Але тепер ми тут у відпустці Ale teper my tut u vidpusttsi
It's so hot!	Яка спека! Yaka speka!
Yes, today it's really hot.	Так, сьогодні дійсно спекотно. Tak, s'ohodni diy̆sno spekotno.
Let's go to the balcony.	Ходімо на балкон. Khodimo na balkon.
There's a party here tomorrow.	Завтра тут буде вечірка. Zavtra tut bude vechirka.
Are you also coming?	Ви також прийдете? Vy takozh pryy̆dete?
Yes, we've also been invited.	Так, ми також запрошені. Tak, my takozh zaprosheni.

23 [twenty-three]

Learning foreign languages

23 [двадцять три]
23 [dvadtsyat' try]

Вивчення іноземних мов

Vyvchennya inozemnykh mov

Where did you learn Spanish?	Де Ви вчили іспанську? De Vy vchyly ispans'ku?
Can you also speak Portuguese?	Ви знаєте також португальську? Vy znayete takozh portuhal's'ku?
Yes, and I also speak some Italian.	Так, я знаю також трошки італійську. Tak, ya znayu takozh troshky italiy̆s'ku.
I think you speak very well.	Я вважаю, що Ви говорите дуже добре. YA vvazhayu, shcho Vy hovoryte duzhe dobre.
The languages are quite similar.	Мови досить подібні. Movy dosyt' podibni.
I can understand them well.	Я їх розумію добре. YA ïkh rozumiyu dobre.
But speaking and writing is difficult.	Але говорити і писати важко. Ale hovoryty i pysaty vazhko.
I still make many mistakes.	Я роблю ще багато помилок. YA roblyu shche bahato pomylok.
Please correct me each time.	Виправляйте мене завжди, будь-ласка. Vypravlyay̆te mene zavzhdy, bud'-laska.

23 [twenty-three]

Learning foreign languages

23 [двадцять три]
23 [dvadtsyat' try]

Вивчення іноземних мов
Vyvchennya inozemnykh mov

Your pronunciation is very good.	Ваша вимова цілком добра. Vasha vymova tsilkom dobra.
You only have a slight accent.	Ви маєте маленький акцент. Vy mayete malen'kyў aktsent.
One can tell where you come from.	Можна дізнатися, звідки Ви родом. Mozhna diznatysya , zvidky Vy rodom.
What is your mother tongue / native language (am.)?	Яка мова є для вас рідною? Yaka mova ye dlya vas ridnoyu?
Are you taking a language course?	Ви відвідуєте мовний курс? Vy vidviduyete movnyў kurs?
Which textbook are you using?	Які навчальні матеріали ви використовуєте? Yaki navchal'ni materialy vy vykorystovuyete?
I don't remember the name right now.	Я зараз не знаю, як це називається. YA zaraz ne znayu, yak tse nazyvayet'sya.
The title is not coming to me.	Я не можу пригадати назви. YA ne mozhu pryhadaty nazvy.
I've forgotten it.	Я це забув / забула. YA tse zabuv / zabula.

24 [twenty-four]

Appointment

24 [двадцять чотири]
24 [dvadtsyat' chotyry]

Домовленість про зустріч
Domovlenist' pro zustrich

Did you miss the bus?	Ти запізнився на автобус? Ty zapiznyvsya na avtobus?
I waited for you for half an hour.	Я чекав на тебе півгодини. YA chekav na tebe pivhodyny.
Don't you have a mobile / cell phone (am.) with you?	Ти не маєш мобільного телефону з собою? Ty ne mayesh mobil'noho telefonu z soboyu?
Be punctual next time!	Будь пунктуальним наступного разу! Bud' punktual'nym nastupnoho razu!
Take a taxi next time!	Візьми наступного разу таксі! Viz'my nastupnoho razu taksi!
Take an umbrella with you next time!	Візьми наступного разу парасольку! Viz'my nastupnoho razu parasol'ku!
I have the day off tomorrow.	Завтра я вільний / вільна. Zavtra ya vil'nyў / vil'na.
Shall we meet tomorrow?	Зустрінемося завтра? Zustrinemosya zavtra?
I'm sorry, I can't make it tomorrow.	На жаль, завтра я не можу. Na zhal', zavtra ya ne mozhu.

24 [twenty-four]

24 [двадцять чотири]
24 [dvadtsyat' chotyry]

Appointment

Домовленість про зустріч
Domovlenist' pro zustrich

Do you already have plans for this weekend?	В тебе вже є плани на ці вихідні? V tebe vzhe ye plany na tsi vykhidni?
Or do you already have an appointment?	Чи в тебе вже є плани? Chy v tebe vzhe ye plany?
I suggest that we meet on the weekend.	Я пропоную зустрітися на вихідних. YA proponuyu zustritysya na vykhidnykh.
Shall we have a picnic?	Влаштуємо пікнік? Vlashtuyemo piknik?
Shall we go to the beach?	Їдемо на пляж? Ïdemo na plyazh?
Shall we go to the mountains?	Їдемо в гори? Ïdemo v hory?
I will pick you up at the office.	Я заберу тебе з офісу. YA zaberu tebe z ofisu.
I will pick you up at home.	Я заберу тебе з дому. YA zaberu tebe z domu.
I will pick you up at the bus stop.	Я заберу тебе на автобусній зупинці. YA zaberu tebe na avtobusniy̆ zupyntsi.

25 [twenty-five]

25 [двадцять п'ять]
25 [dvadtsyat' p"yat']

In the city

У місті
U misti

I would like to go to the station.	Я хотів би / хотіла б на вокзал. YA khotiv by / khotila b na vokzal.
I would like to go to the airport.	Я хотів би / хотіла б до аеропорту. YA khotiv by / khotila b do aeroportu.
I would like to go to the city centre / center (am.).	Я хотів би / хотіла б в центр міста. YA khotiv by / khotila b v tsentr mista.
How do I get to the station?	Як дістатися на вокзал? Yak distatysya na vokzal?
How do I get to the airport?	Як дістатися до аеропорту? Yak distatysya do aeroportu?
How do I get to the city centre / center (am.)?	Як дістатися до центру міста? Yak distatysya do tsentru mista?
I need a taxi.	Мені потрібне таксі. Meni potribne taksi.
I need a city map.	Мені потрібна мапа міста. Meni potribna mapa mista.
I need a hotel.	Мені потрібен готель. Meni potriben hotel'.

25 [twenty-five]

25 [двадцять п’ять]
25 [dvadtsyat’ p”yat’]

In the city

У місті
U misti

I would like to rent a car.
Я хотів би / хотіла б найняти автомобіль.
YA khotiv by / khotila b naÿnyaty avtomobil’.

Here is my credit card.
Ось моя кредитна картка.
Os’ moya kredytna kartka.

Here is my licence / license (am.).
Ось мої права.
Os’ moï prava.

What is there to see in the city?
Що можна оглянути в місті?
Shcho mozhna ohlyanuty v misti?

Go to the old city.
Ідіть в старе місто.
Idit’ v stare misto.

Go on a city tour.
Візьміть участь в екскурсії до міста.
Viz’mit’ uchast’ v ekskursiï do mista.

Go to the harbour / harbor (am.).
Ідіть до порту.
Idit’ do portu.

Go on a harbour / harbor (am.) tour.
Візьміть участь в екскурсії до порту.
Viz’mit’ uchast’ v ekskursiï do portu.

Are there any other places of interest?
Які є ще визначні місця?
Yaki ye shche vyznachni mistsya?

26 [twenty-six]

26 [двадцять шість]
26 [dvadtsyat' shist']

In nature

На природі
Na pryrodi

Do you see the tower there?
Бачиш там вежу?
Bachysh tam vezhu?

Do you see the mountain there?
Бачиш там гору?
Bachysh tam horu?

Do you see the village there?
Бачиш там село?
Bachysh tam selo?

Do you see the river there?
Бачиш там річку?
Bachysh tam richku?

Do you see the bridge there?
Бачиш там міст?
Bachysh tam mist?

Do you see the lake there?
Бачиш там озеро?
Bachysh tam ozero?

I like that bird.
Той птах мені подобається.
Toў ptakh meni podobayet'sya.

I like that tree.
Те дерево мені подобається.
Te derevo meni podobayet'sya.

I like this stone.
Той камінь мені подобається.
Toў kamin' meni podobayet'sya.

26 [twenty-six]

26 [двадцять шість]
26 [dvadtsyat' shist']

In nature

На природі
Na pryrodi

I like that park.	Той парк мені подобається. Toў park meni podobayet'sya.
I like that garden.	Той сад мені подобається. Toў sad meni podobayet'sya.
I like this flower.	Та квітка мені подобається. Ta kvitka meni podobayet'sya.
I find that pretty.	Я вважаю це гарним. YA vvazhayu tse harnym.
I find that interesting.	Я вважаю це цікавим. YA vvazhayu tse tsikavym.
I find that gorgeous.	Я вважаю це чудовим. YA vvazhayu tse chudovym.
I find that ugly.	Я вважаю це бридким. YA vvazhayu tse brydkym.
I find that boring.	Я вважаю це нудним. YA vvazhayu tse nudnym.
I find that terrible.	Я вважаю це страшним. YA vvazhayu tse strashnym.

27 [twenty-seven]

In the hotel – Arrival

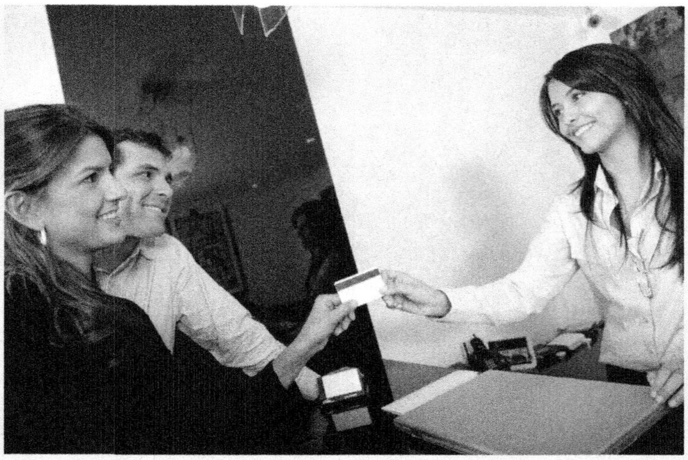

27 [Двадцять сім]
27 [Dvadtsyat' sim]

В готелі – прибуття
V hoteli – prybuttya

Do you have a vacant room?	У вас є вільна кімната? U vas ye vil'na kimnata?
I have booked a room.	Я зарезервував / зарезервувала кімнату. YA zarezervuvav / zarezervuvala kimnatu.
My name is Miller.	Моє ім'я – Мюллер. Moye im"ya – Myuller.
I need a single room.	Мені потрібна окрема кімната. Meni potribna okrema kimnata.
I need a double room.	Мені потрібна кімната для двох. Meni potribna kimnata dlya dvokh.
What does the room cost per night?	Скільки коштує кімната на ніч? Skil'ky koshtuye kimnata na nich?
I would like a room with a bathroom.	Я хочу кімнату з ванною. YA khochu kimnatu z vannoyu.
I would like a room with a shower.	Я хочу кімнату з душем. YA khochu kimnatu z dushem.
Can I see the room?	Чи можу я подивитися на кімнату? Chy mozhu ya podyvytysya na kimnatu?

27 [twenty-seven]

In the hotel – Arrival

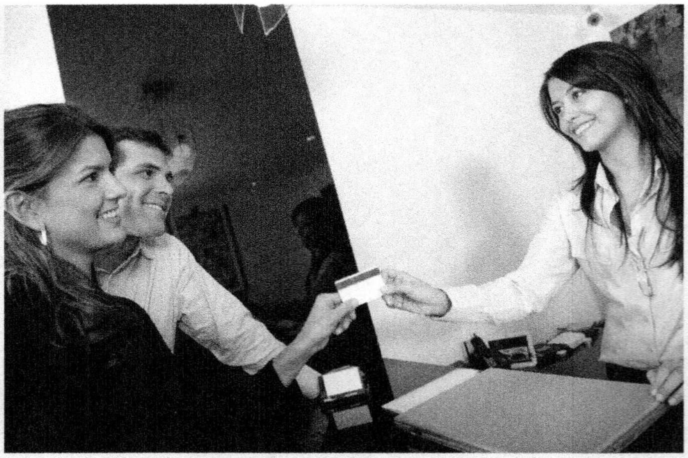

27 [Двадцять сім]
27 [Dvadtsyat' sim]

В готелі – прибуття
V hoteli – prybuttya

Is there a garage here?	Чи є тут гараж? Chy ye tut harazh?
Is there a safe here?	Чи є тут сейф? Chy ye tut seÿf?
Is there a fax machine here?	Чи є тут факс? Chy ye tut faks?
Fine, I'll take the room.	Добре, я беру кімнату. Dobre, ya beru kimnatu.
Here are the keys.	Ось ключі. Os' klyuchi.
Here is my luggage.	Ось мій багаж. Os' miÿ bahazh.
What time do you serve breakfast?	О котрій годині подається сніданок? O kotriÿ hodyni podayet'sya snidanok?
What time do you serve lunch?	О котрій годині подається обід? O kotriÿ hodyni podayet'sya obid?
What time do you serve dinner?	О котрій годині подається вечеря? O kotriÿ hodyni podayet'sya vecherya?

28 [twenty-eight]

In the hotel – Complaints

28 [двадцять вісім]
28 [dvadtsyat' visim]

В готелі – скарги
V hoteli – skarhy

The shower isn't working.	Душ не працює. Dush ne pratsyuye.
There is no warm water.	Теплої води немає. Teploï vody nemaye.
Can you get it repaired?	Чи можете Ви це відремонтувати? Chy mozhete Vy tse vidremontuvaty?
There is no telephone in the room.	У кімнаті немає телефона. U kimnati nemaye telefona.
There is no TV in the room.	У кімнаті немає телевізора. U kimnati nemaye televizora.
The room has no balcony.	У кімнаті немає балкона. U kimnati nemaye balkona.
The room is too noisy.	Кімната надто гучна. Kimnata nadto huchna.
The room is too small.	Кімната надто маленька. Kimnata nadto malen'ka.
The room is too dark.	Кімната надто темна. Kimnata nadto temna.

28 [twenty-eight]

28 [двадцять вісім]
28 [dvadtsyat' visim]

In the hotel – Complaints

В готелі – скарги
V hoteli – skarhy

The heater isn't working.
Опалення не працює.
Opalennya ne pratsyuye.

The air-conditioning isn't working.
Кондиціонер не працює.
Kondytsioner ne pratsyuye.

The TV isn't working.
Телевізор не працює.
Televizor ne pratsyuye.

I don't like that.
Це мені не подобається.
Tse meni ne podobayet'sya.

That's too expensive.
Це для мене задорого.
Tse dlya mene zadoroho.

Do you have anything cheaper?
У вас немає чогось дешевшого?
U vas nemaye chohos' deshevshoho?

Is there a youth hostel nearby?
Тут поблизу є молодіжна туристична база?
Tut poblyzu ye molodizhna turystychna baza?

Is there a boarding house / a bed and breakfast nearby?
Тут поблизу є пансіонат?
Tut poblyzu ye pansionat?

Is there a restaurant nearby?
Тут поблизу є ресторан?
Tut poblyzu ye restoran?

29 [twenty-nine]

29 [двадцять дев’ять]
29 [dvadtsyat’ dev”yat’]

At the restaurant 1

В ресторані 1
V restorani 1

Is this table taken?	Чи цей стіл вільний? Chy tseў stil vil’nyў?
I would like the menu, please.	Я хотів би / хотіла б меню, будь-ласка. YA khotiv by / khotila b menyu, bud’-laska.
What would you recommend?	Що Ви можете порадити? Shcho Vy mozhete poradyty?
I’d like a beer.	Я б випив / випила пиво. YA b vypyv / vypyla pyvo.
I’d like a mineral water.	Я б випив / випила мінеральну воду. YA b vypyv / vypyla mineral’nu vodu.
I’d like an orange juice.	Я б випив / випила помаранчевий сік. YA b vypyv / vypyla pomaranchevyў sik.
I’d like a coffee.	Я б випив / випила каву. YA b vypyv / vypyla kavu.
I’d like a coffee with milk.	Я б випив / випила каву з молоком. YA b vypyv / vypyla kavu z molokom.
With sugar, please.	З цукром, будь-ласка. Z tsukrom, bud’-laska.

29 [twenty-nine]

At the restaurant 1

29 [двадцять дев’ять]
29 [dvadtsyat’ dev”yat’]

В ресторані 1
V restorani 1

I’d like a tea. — Я хочу чаю.
YA khochu chayu.

I’d like a tea with lemon. — Я хочу чаю з лимоном.
YA khochu chayu z lymonom.

I’d like a tea with milk. — Я хочу чаю з молоком.
YA khochu chayu z molokom.

Do you have cigarettes? — Ви маєте цигарки?
Vy mayete tsyharky?

Do you have an ashtray? — Ви маєте попільничку?
Vy mayete popil’nychku?

Do you have a light? — Маєте запальничку?
Mayete zapal’nychku?

I’m missing a fork. — Я не маю виделки.
YA ne mayu vydelky.

I’m missing a knife. — Я не маю ножа.
YA ne mayu nozha.

I’m missing a spoon. — Я не маю ложки.
YA ne mayu lozhky.

30 [thirty]

At the restaurant 2

30 [тридцять]
30 [trydtsyat’]

В ресторані 2
V restorani 2

An apple juice, please.	Яблучний сік, будь-ласка. Yabluchnyǔ sik, bud’-laska.
A lemonade, please.	Лимонад, будь-ласка. Lymonad, bud’-laska.
A tomato juice, please.	Томатний сік, будь-ласка. Tomatnyǔ sik, bud’-laska.
I’d like a glass of red wine.	Я б випив / випила келих червоного вина. YA b vypyv / vypyla kelykh chervonoho vyna.
I’d like a glass of white wine.	Я б випив / випила келих білого вина. YA b vypyv / vypyla kelykh biloho vyna.
I’d like a bottle of champagne.	Мені, будь-ласка, пляшку шампанського. Meni, bud’-laska, plyashku shampans’koho.
Do you like fish?	Ти любиш рибу? Ty lyubysh rybu?
Do you like beef?	Ти любиш яловичину? Ty lyubysh yalovychynu?
Do you like pork?	Ти любиш свинину? Ty lyubysh svynynu?

30 [thirty]

30 [тридцять]
30 [trydtsyat']

At the restaurant 2

В ресторані 2
V restorani 2

I'd like something without meat.
Я хотів би / хотіла б щось без м'яса.
YA khotiv by / khotila b shchos' bez m'yasa.

I'd like some mixed vegetables.
Я хотів би / хотіла б овочеву страву.
YA khotiv by / khotila b ovochevu stravu.

I'd like something that won't take much time.
Я хочу щось, на що не треба довго чекати.
YA khochu shchos', na shcho ne treba dovho chekaty.

Would you like that with rice?
Ви хочете це з рисом?
Vy khochete tse z rysom?

Would you like that with pasta?
Ви хочете це з макаронами?
Vy khochete tse z makaronamy?

Would you like that with potatoes?
Ви хочете це з картоплею?
Vy khochete tse z kartopleyu?

That doesn't taste good.
Це мені не смакує.
Tse meni ne smakuye.

The food is cold.
Їжа холодна.
Їzha kholodna.

I didn't order this.
Я цього не замовляв / замовляла.
YA ts'oho ne zamovlyav / zamovlyala.

31 [thirty-one]

At the restaurant 3

31 [тридцять один]

31 [trydtsyat' odyn]

В ресторані 3

V restorani 3

I would like a starter.	Я хочу закуску. YA khochu zakusku.
I would like a salad.	Я хочу салат. YA khochu salat.
I would like a soup.	Я хочу суп. YA khochu sup.
I would like a dessert.	Я хочу десерт. YA khochu desert.
I would like an ice cream with whipped cream.	Я хочу морозиво з вершками. YA khochu morozyvo z vershkamy.
I would like some fruit or cheese.	Я хочу фрукти або сир. YA khochu frukty abo syr.
We would like to have breakfast.	Ми хочемо снідати. My khochemo snidaty.
We would like to have lunch.	Ми хочемо обідати. My khochemo obidaty.
We would like to have dinner.	Ми хочемо вечеряти. My khochemo vecheryaty.

31 [thirty-one]

31 [тридцять один]
31 [trydtsyat' odyn]

At the restaurant 3

В ресторані 3
V restorani 3

What would you like for breakfast?
Що Ви хочете на сніданок?
Shcho Vy khochete na snidanok?

Rolls with jam and honey?
Булочку з мармеладом і медом?
Bulochku z marmeladom i medom?

Toast with sausage and cheese?
Тост з ковбасою і сиром?
Tost z kovbasoyu i syrom?

A boiled egg?
Варене яйце?
Varene yaӯtse?

A fried egg?
Яєчню?
Yayechnyu?

An omelette?
Омлет?
Omlet?

Another yoghurt, please.
Будь-ласка, ще йогурт.
Bud'-laska, shche ӯohurt.

Some salt and pepper also, please.
Будь-ласка, ще сіль і перець.
Bud'-laska, shche sil' i perets'.

Another glass of water, please.
Будь-ласка, ще склянку води.
Bud'-laska, shche sklyanku vody.

32 [thirty-two]

32 [тридцять два]
32 [trydtsyat' dva]

At the restaurant 4

В ресторані 4
V restorani 4

I'd like chips / French fries (am.) with ketchup.	Одну порцію картоплі фрі з кетчупом. Odnu portsiyu kartopli fri z ketchupom.
And two with mayonnaise.	І дві порції з майонезом. I dvi portsiï z maĭonezom.
And three sausages with mustard.	І три порції смаженої ковбаси з гірчицею. I try portsiï smazhenoï kovbasy z hirchytseyu.
What vegetables do you have?	Що у вас є з овочів? Shcho u vas ye z ovochiv?
Do you have beans?	У вас є квасоля? U vas ye kvasolya?
Do you have cauliflower?	У вас є цвітна капуста? U vas ye tsvitna kapusta?
I like to eat (sweet) corn.	Я їм охоче кукурудзу. YA ïm okhoche kukurudzu.
I like to eat cucumber.	Я їм охоче огірки. YA ïm okhoche ohirky.
I like to eat tomatoes.	Я їм охоче помідори. YA ïm okhoche pomidory.

32 [thirty-two]

At the restaurant 4

32 [тридцять два]
32 [trydtsyat' dva]

В ресторані 4
V restorani 4

Do you also like to eat leek?	Чи їсте Ви також охоче порей? Chy ïste Vy takozh okhoche poreÿ?
Do you also like to eat sauerkraut?	Чи їсте Ви також охоче квашену капусту? Chy ïste Vy takozh okhoche kvashenu kapustu?
Do you also like to eat lentils?	Чи їсте Ви також охоче сочевицю? Chy ïste Vy takozh okhoche sochevytsyu?
Do you also like to eat carrots?	Чи їси ти також охоче моркву? Chy ïsy ty takozh okhoche morkvu?
Do you also like to eat broccoli?	Чи їси ти також охоче броколі? Chy ïsy ty takozh okhoche brokoli?
Do you also like to eat peppers?	Чи їси ти також охоче червоний перець? Chy ïsy ty takozh okhoche chervonyÿ perets'?
I don't like onions.	Я не люблю цибулі. YA ne lyublyu tsybuli.
I don't like olives.	Я не люблю маслин. YA ne lyublyu maslyn.
I don't like mushrooms.	Я не люблю грибів. YA ne lyublyu hrybiv.

33 [thirty-three]

At the train station

33 [тридцять три]
33 [trydtsyat' try]

На вокзалі
Na vokzali

When is the next train to Berlin?
Коли відправляється найближчий потяг до Берліна?
Koly vidpravlyayet'sya naÿblyzhchyÿ potyah do Berlina?

When is the next train to Paris?
Коли відправляється найближчий потяг до Парижа?
Koly vidpravlyayet'sya naÿblyzhchyÿ potyah do Paryzha?

When is the next train to London?
Коли відправляється найближчий потяг до Лондона?
Koly vidpravlyayet'sya naÿblyzhchyÿ potyah do Londona?

When does the train for Warsaw leave?
О котрій годині відправляється потяг до Варшави?
O kotriÿ hodyni vidpravlyayet'sya potyah do Varshavy?

When does the train for Stockholm leave?
О котрій годині відправляється потяг до Стокгольма?
O kotriÿ hodyni vidpravlyayet'sya potyah do Stok•hol'ma?

When does the train for Budapest leave?
О котрій годині відправляється потяг до Будапешта?
O kotriÿ hodyni vidpravlyayet'sya potyah do Budapeshta?

I'd like a ticket to Madrid.
Я хочу квиток до Мадрида.
YA khochu kvytok do Madryda.

I'd like a ticket to Prague.
Я хочу квиток до Праги.
YA khochu kvytok do Prahy.

I'd like a ticket to Bern.
Я хочу квиток до Берну.
YA khochu kvytok do Bernu.

33 [thirty-three]

At the train station

33 [тридцять три]
33 [trydtsyat' try]

На вокзалі
Na vokzali

When does the train arrive in Vienna?	Коли потяг прибуває у Відень? Koly potyah prybuvaye u Viden'?
When does the train arrive in Moscow?	Коли потяг прибуває в Москву? Koly potyah prybuvaye v Moskvu?
When does the train arrive in Amsterdam?	Коли потяг прибуває в Амстердам? Koly potyah prybuvaye v Amsterdam?
Do I have to change trains?	Чи повинен / повинна я пересідати? Chy povynen / povynna ya peresidaty?
From which platform does the train leave?	З якої колії відправляється потяг? Z yakoï koliï vidpravlyayet'sya potyah?
Does the train have sleepers?	Чи є спальний вагон у потязі? Chy ye spal'nyy̆ vahon u potyazi?
I'd like a one-way ticket to Brussels.	Я хочу квиток в один бік до Брюсселя. YA khochu kvytok v odyn bik do Bryusselya.
I'd like a return ticket to Copenhagen.	Я хочу зворотній квиток до Копенгагена. YA khochu zvorotniy̆ kvytok do Kopenhahena.
What does a berth in the sleeper cost?	Скільки коштує місце в спальному вагоні? Skil'ky koshtuye mistse v spal'nomu vahoni?

34 [thirty-four]

On the train

34 [тридцять чотири]
34 [trydtsyat' chotyry]

У поїзді
U poïzdi

Is that the train to Berlin?	Це потяг до Берліна? Tse potyah do Berlina?
When does the train leave?	Коли відправляється потяг? Koly vidpravlyayet'sya potyah?
When does the train arrive in Berlin?	Коли прибуває потяг до Берліна? Koly prybuvaye potyah do Berlina?
Excuse me, may I pass?	Пробачте, можна пройти? Probachte, mozhna proÿty?
I think this is my seat.	Мені здається, це – моє місце. Meni zdayet'sya, tse – moye mistse.
I think you're sitting in my seat.	Мені здається, Ви сидите на моєму місці. Meni zdayet'sya, Vy sydyte na moyemu mistsi.
Where is the sleeper?	Де спальний вагон? De spal'nyÿ vahon?
The sleeper is at the end of the train.	Спальний вагон у кінці потягу. Spal'nyÿ vahon u kintsi potyahu.
And where is the dining car? – At the front.	А де вагон – ресторан? – На початку поїзда. A de vahon – restoran? – Na pochatku poïzda.

34 [thirty-four]

34 [тридцять чотири]
34 [trydtsyat' chotyry]

On the train

У поїзді
U poïzdi

Can I sleep below?
Можна мені спати на нижній полиці?
Mozhna meni spaty na nyzhniÿ polytsi?

Can I sleep in the middle?
Можна мені спати посередині?
Mozhna meni spaty poseredyni?

Can I sleep at the top?
Можна мені спати на верхній полиці?
Mozhna meni spaty na verkhniÿ polytsi?

When will we get to the border?
Коли ми будемо на кордоні?
Koly my budemo na kordoni?

How long does the journey to Berlin take?
Як довго триває поїздка до Берліна?
Yak dovho tryvaye poïzdka do Berlina?

Is the train delayed?
Чи потяг запізнюється?
Chy potyah zapiznyuyet'sya?

Do you have something to read?
Чи маєте Ви щось почитати?
Chy mayete Vy shchos' pochytaty?

Can one get something to eat and to drink here?
Тут можна поїсти та попити?
Tut mozhna poïsty ta popyty?

Could you please wake me up at 7 o'clock?
Можете мене розбудити, будь-ласка, о 7.00 годині?
Mozhete mene rozbudyty, bud'-laska, o 7.00 hodyni?

35 [thirty-five]

35 [тридцять п’ять]
35 [trydtsyat’ p”yat’]

At the airport

В аеропорту
V aeroportu

I’d like to book a flight to Athens.
Я хотів би / хотіла би забронювати квиток до Афін.
YA khotiv by / khotila by zabronyuvaty kvytok do Afin.

Is it a direct flight?
Це прямий рейс?
Tse pryamyy̆ rey̆s?

A window seat, non-smoking, please.
Будь-ласка, місце біля вікна, для некурящих.
Bud’-laska, mistse bilya vikna, dlya nekuryashchykh.

I would like to confirm my reservation.
Я хотів би / хотіла би підтвердити мою броню.
YA khotiv by / khotila by pidtverdyty moyu bronyu.

I would like to cancel my reservation.
Я хотів би / хотіла би скасувати мою броню.
YA khotiv by / khotila by skasuvaty moyu bronyu.

I would like to change my reservation.
Я хотів би / хотіла би перенести замовлення моєї броні.
YA khotiv by / khotila by perenesty zamovlennya moyeï broni.

When is the next flight to Rome?
Коли найближчий рейс до Риму?
Koly nay̆blyzhchyy̆ rey̆s do Rymu?

Are there two seats available?
Є ще два вільних місця?
YE shche dva vil’nykh mistsya?

No, we have only one seat available.
Ні, є лише одне вільне місце.
Ni, ye lyshe odne vil’ne mistse.

35 [thirty-five]

35 [тридцять п’ять]
35 [trydtsyat’ p”yat’]

At the airport

В аеропорту
V aeroportu

When do we land?
Коли ми приземляємося?
Koly my pryzemlyayemosya?

When will we be there?
Коли ми прибуваємо?
Koly my prybuvayemo?

When does a bus go to the city centre / center (am.)?
Коли їздить автобус в центр міста?
Koly ïzdyt’ avtobus v tsentr mista?

Is that your suitcase?
Це Ваша валіза?
Tse Vasha valiza?

Is that your bag?
Це Ваша сумка?
Tse Vasha sumka?

Is that your luggage?
Це Ваш багаж?
Tse Vash bahazh?

How much luggage can I take?
Як багато багажу я можу взяти?
Yak bahato bahazhu ya mozhu vzyaty?

Twenty kilos.
Двадцять кілограм.
Dvadtsyat’ kilohram.

What? Only twenty kilos?
Що, тільки двадцять кілограм?
Shcho, til’ky dvadtsyat’ kilohram?

36 [thirty-six]

Public transportation

36 [тридцять шість]

36 [trydtsyat' shist']

Приміське сполучення

Prymis'ke spoluchennya

Where is the bus stop?	Де автобусна зупинка? De avtobusna zupynka?
Which bus goes to the city centre / center (am.)?	Який автобус їздить в центр? Yakyÿ avtobus ïzdyt' v tsentr?
Which bus do I have to take?	Якою лінією мені їхати? Yakoyu liniyeyu meni ïkhaty?
Do I have to change?	Чи повинен / повинна я пересідати? Chy povynen / povynna ya peresidaty?
Where do I have to change?	Де я повинен / повинна пересісти? De ya povynen / povynna peresisty?
How much does a ticket cost?	Скільки коштує проїзний квиток? Skil'ky koshtuye proïznyÿ kvytok?
How many stops are there before downtown / the city centre?	Як багато зупинок до центру? Yak bahato zupynok do tsentru?
You have to get off here.	Ви повинні тут вийти. Vy povynni tut vyÿty.
You have to get off at the back.	Ви повинні вийти ззаду. Vy povynni vyÿty zzadu.

36 [thirty-six]

Public transportation

36 [тридцять шість]
36 [trydtsyat' shist']

Приміське сполучення
Prymis'ke spoluchennya

The next train is in 5 minutes.	Наступне метро прибуває через 5 хвилин. Nastupne metro prybuvaye cherez 5 khvylyn.
The next tram is in 10 minutes.	Наступний трамвай прибуває через 10 хвилин. Nastupnyў tramvaў prybuvaye cherez 10 khvylyn.
The next bus is in 15 minutes.	Наступний автобус прибуває через 15 хвилин. Nastupnyў avtobus prybuvaye cherez 15 khvylyn.
When is the last train?	Коли відправляється останнє метро? Koly vidpravlyayet'sya ostannye metro?
When is the last tram?	Коли відправляється останній трамвай? Koly vidpravlyayet'sya ostanniў tramvaў?
When is the last bus?	Коли відправляється останній автобус? Koly vidpravlyayet'sya ostanniў avtobus?
Do you have a ticket?	Маєте квиток на проїзд? Mayete kvytok na proïzd?
A ticket? – No, I don't have one.	Квиток на проїзд? – Ні, я не маю. Kvytok na proïzd? – Ni, ya ne mayu.
Then you have to pay a fine.	Тоді Ви повинні заплатити штраф. Todi Vy povynni zaplatyty shtraf.

37 [thirty-seven]

En route

37 [тридцять сім]
37 [trydtsyat' sim]

В дорозі
V dorozi

He drives a motorbike.	Він їде на мотоциклі. Vin ïde na mototsykli.
He rides a bicycle.	Він їде на велосипеді. Vin ïde na velosypedi.
He walks.	Він йде пішки. Vin ỹde pishky.
He goes by ship.	Він пливе на кораблі. Vin plyve na korabli.
He goes by boat.	Він пливе на човні. Vin plyve na chovni.
He swims.	Він пливе. Vin plyve.
Is it dangerous here?	Чи тут небезпечно? Chy tut nebezpechno?
Is it dangerous to hitchhike alone?	Чи небезпечно самому / самій подорожувати? Chy nebezpechno samomu / samiỹ podorozhuvaty?
Is it dangerous to go for a walk at night?	Чи небезпечно вночі самому / самій гуляти? Chy nebezpechno vnochi samomu / samiỹ hulyaty?

37 [thirty-seven]

37 [тридцять сім]
37 [trydtsyat' sim]

En route

В дорозі
V dorozi

We got lost.
Ми заблукали.
My zablukaly.

We're on the wrong road.
Ми на неправильному шляху.
My na nepravyl'nomu shlyakhu.

We must turn around.
Ми повинні повернутися.
My povynni povernutysya.

Where can one park here?
Де можна тут припаркуватися?
De mozhna tut pryparkuvatysya?

Is there a parking lot here?
Чи є тут місце для парковки?
Chy ye tut mistse dlya parkovky?

How long can one park here?
Як довго можна тут стояти?
Yak dovho mozhna tut stoyaty?

Do you ski?
Ви катаєтесь на лижах?
Vy katayetes' na lyzhakh?

Do you take the ski lift to the top?
Ви їдете на лижному ліфті вгору?
Vy ïdete na lyzhnomu lifti vhoru?

Can one rent skis here?
Тут можна взяти лижі в прокат?
Tut mozhna vzyaty lyzhi v prokat?

38 [thirty-eight]

38 [тридцять вісім]
38 [trydtsyat' visim]

In the taxi

У таксі
U taksi

Please call a taxi.
Викличте, будь-ласка, таксі.
Vyklychte, bud'-laska, taksi.

What does it cost to go to the station?
Скільки коштує до вокзалу?
Skil'ky koshtuye do vokzalu?

What does it cost to go to the airport?
Скільки коштує до аеропорту?
Skil'ky koshtuye do aeroportu?

Please go straight ahead.
Будь-ласка, прямо.
Bud'-laska, pryamo.

Please turn right here.
Будь-ласка, тут праворуч.
Bud'-laska, tut pravoruch.

Please turn left at the corner.
Будь-ласка, там на розі ліворуч.
Bud'-laska, tam na rozi livoruch.

I'm in a hurry.
Я поспішаю.
YA pospishayu.

I have time.
Я маю час.
YA mayu chas.

Please drive slowly.
Їдьте, будь-ласка, повільніше.
Ïd'te, bud'-laska, povil'nishe.

38 [thirty-eight]

38 [тридцять вісім]
38 [trydtsyat' visim]

In the taxi

У таксі
U taksi

Please stop here.	Зупиніться тут, будь-ласка. Zupynit'sya tut, bud'-laska.
Please wait a moment.	Зачекайте хвилинку, будь-ласка. Zachekaўte khvylynku, bud'-laska.
I'll be back immediately.	Я зараз повернуся. YA zaraz povernusya.
Please give me a receipt.	Дайте мені, будь-ласка, чек. Daўte meni, bud'-laska, chek.
I have no change.	В мене немає дрібних грошей. V mene nemaye dribnykh hrosheў.
That is okay, please keep the change.	Достатньо, решта для вас. Dostatn'o, reshta dlya vas.
Drive me to this address.	Відвезіть мене за цією адресою. Vidvezit' mene za tsiyeyu adresoyu.
Drive me to my hotel.	Відвезіть мене до мого готелю. Vidvezit' mene do moho hotelyu.
Drive me to the beach.	Відвезіть мене на пляж. Vidvezit' mene na plyazh.

39 [thirty-nine]

39 [тридцять дев'ять]
39 [trydtsyat' dev"yat']

Car breakdown

Автопригоди
Avtopryhody

Where is the next gas station?	Де найближча бензоколонка? De naӳblyzhcha benzokolonka?
I have a flat tyre / tire (am.).	В мене пробите колесо. V mene probyte koleso.
Can you change the tyre / tire (am.)?	Чи можете Ви поміняти колесо? Chy mozhete Vy pominyaty koleso?
I need a few litres / liters (am.) of diesel.	Мені потрібні кілька літрів дизельного пального. Meni potribni kil'ka litriv dyzel'noho pal'noho.
I have no more petrol / gas (am.).	В мене закінчилось пальне. V mene zakinchylos' pal'ne.
Do you have a petrol can / jerry can / gas can (am.)?	Чи Маєте ви запасну каністру? Chy Mayete vy zapasnu kanistru?
Where can I make a call?	Звідки я можу зателефонувати? Zvidky ya mozhu zatelefonuvaty?
I need a towing service.	Мені потрібна буксирна служба. Meni potribna buksyrna sluzhba.
I'm looking for a garage.	Я шукаю автосервіс. YA shukayu avtoservis.

39 [thirty-nine]

39 [тридцять дев’ять]
39 [trydtsyat’ dev”yat’]

Car breakdown

Автопригоди
Avtopryhody

An accident has occurred.	Тут трапилася аварія. Tut trapylasya avariya.
Where is the nearest telephone?	Де є найближчий телефон? De ye naўblyzhchyў telefon?
Do you have a mobile / cell phone (am.) with you?	Маєте при собі мобільний телефон? Mayete pry sobi mobil’nyў telefon?
We need help.	Нам потрібна допомога. Nam potribna dopomoha.
Call a doctor!	Викличте лікаря! Vyklychte likarya!
Call the police!	Викличте міліцію! Vyklychte militsiyu!
Your papers, please.	Ваші документи, будь-ласка. Vashi dokumenty, bud’-laska.
Your licence / license (am.), please.	Ваші права, будь-ласка. Vashi prava, bud’-laska.
Your registration, please.	Ваш техпаспорт, будь-ласка. Vash tekhpasport, bud’-laska.

40 [forty]

Asking for directions

40 [сорок]
40 [sorok]

Запитання шляху
Zapytannya shlyakhu

Excuse me!	Вибачте! Vybachte!
Can you help me?	Чи Можете ви мені допомогти? Chy Mozhete vy meni dopomohty?
Is there a good restaurant around here?	Де тут є хороший ресторан? De tut ye khoroshyў restoran?
Take a left at the corner.	Зверніть ліворуч за рогом. Zvernit' livoruch za rohom.
Then go straight for a while.	Йдіть потім прямо. Ўdit' potim pryamo.
Then go right for a hundred metres / meters (am.).	Звернувши праворуч, пройдіть сто метрів. Zvernuvshy pravoruch, proўdit' sto metriv.
You can also take the bus.	Ви можете також поїхати автобусом. Vy mozhete takozh poïkhaty avtobusom.
You can also take the tram.	Ви можете також поїхати трамваєм. Vy mozhete takozh poïkhaty tramvayem.
You can also follow me with your car.	Ви можете також просто поїхати за мною. Vy mozhete takozh prosto poïkhaty za mnoyu.

40 [forty]

Asking for directions

40 [сорок]
40 [sorok]

Запитання шляху
Zapytannya shlyakhu

How do I get to the football / soccer (am.) stadium?	Як пройти до футбольного стадіону? Yak proy̆ty do futbol'noho stadionu?
Cross the bridge!	Перейдіть через міст! Perey̆dit' cherez mist!
Go through the tunnel!	Їдьте через тунель! Ïd'te cherez tunel'!
Drive until you reach the third traffic light.	Їдьте до третього світлофора. Ïd'te do tret'oho svitlofora.
Then turn into the first street on your right.	Зверніть потім у першу вулицю праворуч. Zvernit' potim u pershu vulytsyu pravoruch.
Then drive straight through the next intersection.	Їдьте потім прямо через найближче перехрестя. Ïd'te potim pryamo cherez nay̆blyzhche perekhrestya.
Excuse me, how do I get to the airport?	Вибачте, як потрапити до аеропорту? Vybachte, yak potrapyty do aeroportu?
It is best if you take the underground / subway (am.).	Найкраще на метро. Nay̆krashche na metro.
Simply get out at the last stop.	Їдьте просто до кінцевої зупинки. Ïd'te prosto do kintsevoï zupynky.

41 [forty-one]

41 [сорок один]
41 [sorok odyn]

Where is ... ?

Орієнтування
Oriyentuvannya

Where is the tourist information office?	Де розташоване туристичне бюро? De roztashovane turystychne byuro?
Do you have a city map for me?	У вас є мапа міста для мене? U vas ye mapa mista dlya mene?
Can one reserve a room here?	Можна тут забронювати номер в готелі? Mozhna tut zabronyuvaty nomer v hoteli?
Where is the old city?	Де знаходиться старе місто? De znakhodyt'sya stare misto?
Where is the cathedral?	Де знаходиться кафедральний собор? De znakhodyt'sya kafedral'nyў sobor?
Where is the museum?	Де знаходиться музей? De znakhodyt'sya muzeў?
Where can one buy stamps?	Де можна купити поштові марки? De mozhna kupyty poshtovi marky?
Where can one buy flowers?	Де можна купити квіти? De mozhna kupyty kvity?
Where can one buy tickets?	Де можна купити квитки? De mozhna kupyty kvytky?

41 [forty-one]

Where is ... ?

41 [сорок один]
41 [sorok odyn]

Орієнтування
Oriyentuvannya

Where is the harbour / harbor (am.)?	Де знаходиться порт? De znakhodyt'sya port?
Where is the market?	Де знаходиться базар? De znakhodyt'sya bazar?
Where is the castle?	Де знаходиться замок? De znakhodyt'sya zamok?
When does the tour begin?	Коли починається екскурсія? Koly pochynayet'sya ekskursiya?
When does the tour end?	Коли закінчується екскурсія? Koly zakinchuyet'sya ekskursiya?
How long is the tour?	Як довго триває екскурсія? Yak dovho tryvaye ekskursiya?
I would like a guide who speaks German.	Мені потрібен екскурсовод, який говорить німецькою мовою. Meni potriben ekskursovod, yakyў hovoryt' nimets'koyu movoyu.
I would like a guide who speaks Italian.	Мені потрібен екскурсовод, який говорить італійською. Meni potriben ekskursovod, yakyў hovoryt' italiўs'koyu.
I would like a guide who speaks French.	Мені потрібен екскурсовод, який говорить французькою. Meni potriben ekskursovod, yakyў hovoryt' frantsuz'koyu.

42 [forty-two]

42 [сорок два]
42 [sorok dva]

City tour

Екскурсія до міста
Ekskursiya do mista

Is the market open on Sundays?	Чи відкритий ринок щонеділі? Chy vidkrytyў pynok shchonedili?
Is the fair open on Mondays?	Чи відкритий Ярмарок щопонеділка Chy vidkrytyў Yarmarok shchoponedilka
Is the exhibition open on Tuesdays?	Чи відкрита виставка щовівтірка? Chy vidkryta vystavka shchovivtirka?
Is the zoo open on Wednesdays?	Чи відкритий зоопарк щосереди? Chy vidkrytyў zoopark shchoseredy?
Is the museum open on Thursdays?	Чи відкритий музей щочетверга? Chy vidkrytyў muzeў shchochetverha?
Is the gallery open on Fridays?	Чи відкрита галерея щоп’ятниці? Chy vidkryta halereya shchop'yatnytsi?
Can one take photographs?	Чи можна фотографувати? Chy mozhna fotohrafuvaty?
Does one have to pay an entrance fee?	Чи потрібно платити за вхід? Chy potribno platyty za vkhid?
How much is the entrance fee?	Скільки коштує вхід? Skil’ky koshtuye vkhid?

42 [forty-two]

42 [сорок два]
42 [sorok dva]

City tour

Екскурсія до міста
Ekskursiya do mista

Is there a discount for groups?	Чи є знижка для груп? Chy ye znyzhka dlya hrup?
Is there a discount for children?	Чи є знижка для дітей? Chy ye znyzhka dlya diteў?
Is there a discount for students?	Чи є знижка для студентів? Chy ye znyzhka dlya studentiv?
What building is that?	Що це за будівля? Shcho tse za budivlya?
How old is the building?	Скільки років цій будівлі? Skil'ky rokiv tsiў budivli?
Who built the building?	Хто побудував цю будівлю? Khto pobuduvav tsyu budivlyu?
I'm interested in architecture.	Я цікавлюся архітектурою. YA tsikavlyusya arkhitekturoyu.
I'm interested in art.	Я цікавлюся мистецтвом. YA tsikavlyusya mystetstvom.
I'm interested in paintings.	Я цікавлюся живописом. YA tsikavlyusya zhyvopysom.

43 [forty-three]

At the zoo

43 [сорок три]
43 [sorok try]

В зоопарку
V zooparku

The zoo is there.	Там є зоопарк. Tam ye zoopark.
The giraffes are there.	Там є жирафи. Tam ye zhyrafy.
Where are the bears?	Де є ведмеді? De ye vedmedi?
Where are the elephants?	Де є слони? De ye slony?
Where are the snakes?	Де є змії? De ye zmiï?
Where are the lions?	Де є леви? De ye levy?
I have a camera.	Я маю фотоапарат. YA mayu fotoaparat.
I also have a video camera.	Я маю також відеокамеру. YA mayu takozh videokameru.
Where can I find a battery?	Де є батарея? De ye batareya?

43 [forty-three]

43 [сорок три]
43 [sorok try]

At the zoo

В зоопарку
V zooparku

Where are the penguins?	Де є пінгвіни? De ye pinhviny?
Where are the kangaroos?	Де є кенгуру? De ye kenhuru?
Where are the rhinos?	Де є носороги? De ye nosorohy?
Where is the toilet / restroom (am.)?	Де є туалет? De ye tualet?
There is a café over there.	Там є кафе. Tam ye kafe.
There is a restaurant over there.	Там є ресторан. Tam ye restoran.
Where are the camels?	Де є верблюди? De ye verblyudy?
Where are the gorillas and the zebras?	Де є горили і зебри? De ye horyly i zebry?
Where are the tigers and the crocodiles?	Де є тигри і крокодили? De ye tyhry i krokodyly?

44 [forty-four]

Going out in the evening

44 [сорок чотири]
44 [sorok chotyry]

Вечірні розваги
Vechirni rozvahy

Is there a disco here?	Тут є дискотека? Tut ye dyskoteka?
Is there a nightclub here?	Тут є нічний клуб? Tut ye nichnyў klub?
Is there a pub here?	Тут є пивна? Tut ye pyvna?
What's playing at the theatre / theater (am.) this evening?	Що сьогодні ввечері в театрі? Shcho s'ohodni vvecheri v teatri?
What's playing at the cinema / movies (am.) this evening?	Що сьогодні ввечері в кіно? Shcho s'ohodni vvecheri v kino?
What's on TV this evening?	Що сьогодні ввечері на телебаченні? Shcho s'ohodni vvecheri na telebachenni?
Are tickets for the theatre / theater (am.) still available?	Є ще квитки в театр? YE shche kvytky v teatr?
Are tickets for the cinema / movies (am.) still available?	Є ще квитки в кіно? YE shche kvytky v kino?
Are tickets for the football / soccer am. game still available?	Є ще квитки на футбол? YE shche kvytky na futbol?

44 [forty-four]

Going out in the evening

44 [сорок чотири]
44 [sorok chotyry]

Вечірні розваги
Vechirni rozvahy

I want to sit in the back.	Я хотів би / хотіла б сидіти ззаду. YA khotiv by / khotila b sydity zzadu.
I want to sit somewhere in the middle.	Я хотів би / хотіла б сидіти де-небудь посередині. YA khotiv by / khotila b sydity de-nebud' poseredyni.
I want to sit at the front.	Я хотів би / хотіла б сидіти спереду. YA khotiv by / khotila b sydity speredu.
Could you recommend something?	Що ви можете мені порекомендувати? Shcho vy mozhete meni porekomenduvaty?
When does the show begin?	Коли починається вистава? Koly pochynayet'sya vystava?
Can you get me a ticket?	Чи можете ви купити мені квиток? Chy mozhete vy kupyty meni kvytok?
Is there a golf course nearby?	Тут є неподалік гольф клуб? Tut ye nepodalik hol'f klub?
Is there a tennis court nearby?	Тут є неподалік тенісний корт? Tut ye nepodalik tenisnyŷ kort?
Is there an indoor swimming pool nearby?	Тут є неподалік басейн? Tut ye nepodalik baseŷn?

45 [forty-five]

45 [сорок п’ять]
45 [sorok p”yat’]

At the cinema

В кіно
V kino

We want to go to the cinema.
Ми хочемо в кіно.
My khochemo v kino.

A good film is playing today.
Сьогодні йде хороший фільм.
S’ohodni ўde khoroshyў fil’m.

The film is brand new.
Фільм цілком новий.
Fil’m tsilkom novyў.

Where is the cash register?
Де (є) каса?
De (ye) kasa?

Are seats still available?
Чи є ще вільні місця?
Chy ye shche vil’ni mistsya?

How much are the admission tickets?
Скільки коштують квитки?
Skil’ky koshtuyut’ kvytky?

When does the show begin?
Коли починається сеанс?
Koly pochynayet’sya seans?

How long is the film?
Як довго триває фільм?
Yak dovho tryvaye fil’m?

Can one reserve tickets?
Можна зарезервувати квиток?
Mozhna zarezervuvaty kvytok?

45 [forty-five]

45 [сорок п’ять]

45 [sorok p”yat’]

At the cinema

В кіно

V kino

I want to sit at the back.	Я хотів би / хотіла б сидіти ззаду. YA khotiv by / khotila b sydity zzadu.
I want to sit at the front.	Я хотів би / хотіла б сидіти спереду. YA khotiv by / khotila b sydity speredu.
I want to sit in the middle.	Я хотів би / хотіла б сидіти посередині. YA khotiv by / khotila b sydity poseredyni.
The film was exciting.	Фільм був захоплюючим. Fil’m buv zakhoplyuyuchym.
The film was not boring.	Фільм не був нудний. Fil’m ne buv nudnyў.
But the book on which the film was based was better.	Але книга краща за фільм. Ale knyha krashcha za fil’m.
How was the music?	Яка була музика? Yaka bula muzyka?
How were the actors?	Які були актори? Yaki buly aktory?
Were there English subtitles?	Чи були субтитри англійською мовою? Chy buly subtytry anhliўs’koyu movoyu?

46 [forty-six]

In the discotheque

46 [сосок шість]
46 [sosok shist’]

На дискотеці
Na dyskotetsi

Is this seat taken?	Це місце вільне? Tse mistse vil’ne?
May I sit with you?	Можна сісти біля Вас? Mozhna sisty bilya Vas?
Sure.	Із задоволенням Iz zadovolennyam
How do you like the music?	Чи подобається вам музика? Chy podobayet’sya vam muzyka?
A little too loud.	Трохи заголосно. Trokhy zaholosno.
But the band plays very well.	Але цей гурт грає цілком добре. Ale tseŷ hurt hraye tsilkom dobre.
Do you come here often?	Ви тут часто буваєте? Vy tut chasto buvayete?
No, this is the first time.	Ні, це перший раз. Ni, tse pershyŷ raz.
I’ve never been here before.	Я ще ніколи тут не був / була. YA shche nikoly tut ne buv / bula.

46 [forty-six]

In the discotheque

46 [сорок шість]
46 [sorok shist']

На дискотеці
Na dyskotetsi

Would you like to dance?	Ви танцюєте? Vy tantsyuyete?
Maybe later.	Можливо пізніше. Mozhlyvo piznishe.
I can't dance very well.	Я танцюю не дуже добре. YA tantsyuyu ne duzhe dobre.
It's very easy.	Це зовсім просто. Tse zovsim prosto.
I'll show you.	Я Вам покажу. YA Vam pokazhu.
No, maybe some other time.	Ні, краще іншим разом. Ni, krashche inshym razom.
Are you waiting for someone?	Ви чекаєте на когось? Vy chekayete na kohos'?
Yes, for my boyfriend.	Так, на мого друга. Tak, na moho druha.
There he is!	Ось і він! Os' i vin!

47 [forty-seven]

Preparing a trip

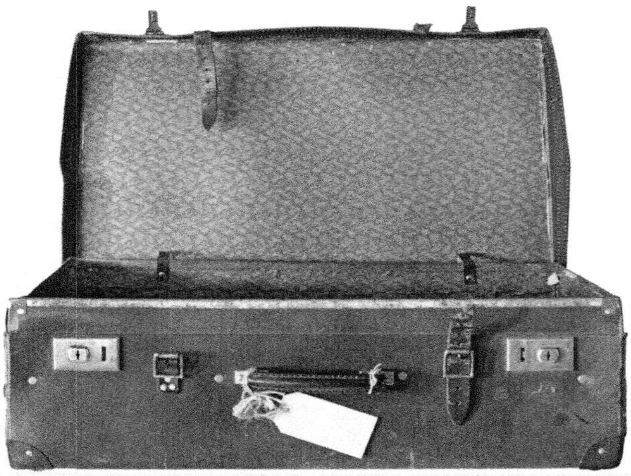

47 [сорок сім]
47 [sorok sim]

Підготовка до подорожі
Pidhotovka do podorozhi

You have to pack our suitcase!	Ти повинен спакувати нашу валізу! Ty povynen spakuvaty nashu valizu!
Don't forget anything!	Ти не повинен нічого забути! Ty ne povynen nichoho zabuty!
You need a big suitcase!	Тобі потрібна велика валіза! Tobi potribna velyka valiza!
Don't forget your passport!	Не забудь закордонний паспорт! Ne zabud' zakordonnyў pasport!
Don't forget your ticket!	Не забудь квиток на літак! Ne zabud' kvytok na litak!
Don't forget your traveller's cheques / traveler's checks (am.)!	Не забудь дорожні чеки! Ne zabud' dorozhni cheky!
Take some suntan lotion with you.	Візьми крем від сонця. Viz'my krem vid sontsya.
Take the sun-glasses with you.	Візьми окуляри від сонця. Viz'my okulyary vid sontsya.
Take the sun hat with you.	Візьми капелюх від сонця. Viz'my kapelyukh vid sontsya.

47 [forty-seven]

Preparing a trip

47 [сорок сім]
47 [sorok sim]

Підготовка до подорожі
Pidhotovka do podorozhi

Do you want to take a road map?	Хочеш взяти мапу доріг? Khochesh vzyaty mapu dorih?
Do you want to take a travel guide?	Хочеш взяти путівник? Khochesh vzyaty putivnyk?
Do you want to take an umbrella?	Хочеш взяти парасольку? Khochesh vzyaty parasol'ku?
Remember to take pants, shirts and socks.	Не забудь взяти штани, сорочки, шкарпетки. Ne zabud' vzyaty shtany, sorochky, shkarpetky.
Remember to take ties, belts and sports jackets.	Не забудь взяти краватки, пояси, жакети. Ne zabud' vzyaty kravatky, poyasy, zhakety.
Remember to take pyjamas, nightgowns and t-shirts.	Не забудь взяти піжами, нічні сорочки, футболки. Ne zabud' vzyaty pizhamy, nichni sorochky, futbolky.
You need shoes, sandals and boots.	Тобі потрібні черевики, сандалі та чоботи. Tobi potribni cherevyky, sandali ta choboty.
You need handkerchiefs, soap and a nail clipper.	Тобі потрібні носові хустинки, мило і манікюрні ножиці. Tobi potribni nosovi khustynky, mylo i manikyurni nozhytsi.
You need a comb, a toothbrush and toothpaste.	Тобі потрібні гребінець, зубна щітка і зубна паста. Tobi potribni hrebinets', zubna shchitka i zubna pasta.

48 [forty-eight]

48 [сорок вісім]
48 [sorok visim]

Vacation activities

Що ми робимо у відпустці

Shcho my robymo u vidpusttsi

Is the beach clean?

Пляж чистий?
Plyazh chystyў?

Can one swim there?

Можна там купатися?
Mozhna tam kupatysya?

Isn't it dangerous to swim there?

Там небезпечно купатися?
Tam nebezpechno kupatysya?

Can one rent a sun umbrella / parasol here?

Можна тут взяти парасольку на прокат?
Mozhna tut vzyaty parasol'ku na prokat?

Can one rent a deck chair here?

Можна тут взяти шезлонг на прокат?
Mozhna tut vzyaty shezlonh na prokat?

Can one rent a boat here?

Можна тут взяти човен на прокат?
Mozhna tut vzyaty choven na prokat?

I would like to surf.

Я б охоче зайнявся / зайнялася серфінгом.
YA b okhoche zaўnyavsya / zaўnyalasya serfinhom.

I would like to dive.

Я б охоче попірнав / попірнала.
YA b okhoche popirnav / popirnala.

I would like to water ski.

Я б охоче покатався / покаталася на водних лижах.
YA b okhoche pokatavsya / pokatalasya na vodnykh lyzhakh.

48 [forty-eight]

Vacation activities

48 [сорок вісім]
48 [sorok visim]

Що ми робимо у відпустці
Shcho my robymo u vidpusttsi

Can one rent a surfboard?	Можна тут взяти на прокат дошку для серфінгу? Mozhna tut vzyaty na prokat doshku dlya serfinhu?
Can one rent diving equipment?	Можна тут взяти на прокат водолазне спорядження? Mozhna tut vzyaty na prokat vodolazne sporyadzhennya?
Can one rent water skis?	Можна тут взяти на прокат водні лижі? Mozhna tut vzyaty na prokat vodni lyzhi?
I'm only a beginner.	Я тільки початківець. YA til'ky pochatkivets'.
I'm moderately good.	Я у цьому трохи обізнаний / обізнана. YA u ts'omu trokhy obiznanyў / obiznana.
I'm pretty good at it.	Я знаюся на цьому. YA znayusya na ts'omu.
Where is the ski lift?	Де лижний підйомник? De lyzhnyў pidўomnyk?
Do you have skis?	Чи маєш ти при собі лижі? Chy mayesh ty pry sobi lyzhi?
Do you have ski boots?	Чи маєш ти при собі лижні черевики? Chy mayesh ty pry sobi lyzhni cherevyky?

49 [forty-nine]

Sports

49 [сорок дев’ять]
49 [sorok dev”yat’]

Спорт

Sport

Do you exercise?	Ти займаєшся спортом? Ty zaÿmayeshsya sportom?
Yes, I need some exercise.	Так, я повинен / повинна рухатися. Tak, ya povynen / povynna rukhatysya.
I am a member of a sports club.	Я ходжу до спортивного клубу. YA khodzhu do sportyvnoho klubu.
We play football / soccer (am.).	Ми граємо у футбол. My hrayemo u futbol.
We swim sometimes.	Іноді ми плаваємо. Inodi my plavayemo.
Or we cycle.	Або ми катаємось на велосипедах. Abo my katayemos’ na velosypedakh.
There is a football / soccer (am.) stadium in our city.	У нашому місті є футбольний стадіон. U nashomu misti ye futbol’nyÿ stadion.
There is also a swimming pool with a sauna.	Є також басейн і сауна. YE takozh baseÿn i sauna.
And there is a golf course.	І є місце для гольфу. I ye mistse dlya hol’fu.

49 [forty-nine]

49 [сорок дев’ять]
49 [sorok dev”yat’]

Sports

Спорт
Sport

What is on TV?

Що йде на телебаченні?
Shcho ÿde na telebachenni?

There is a football / soccer (am.) match on now.

Саме йде футбольний матч.
Same ÿde futbol’nyÿ match.

The German team is playing against the English one.

Німецька команда грає проти англійської.
Nimets’ka komanda hraye proty anhliÿs’koï.

Who is winning?

Хто виграє?
Khto vyhraye?

I have no idea.

Я не знаю.
YA ne znayu.

It is currently a tie.

Поки що нічия.
Poky shcho nichyya.

The referee is from Belgium.

Арбітр з Бельгії.
Arbitr z Bel’hiï.

Now there is a penalty.

Зараз буде пенальті.
Zaraz bude penal’ti.

Goal! One – zero!

Гол! Один: нуль!
Hol! Odyn: nul’!

50 [fifty]

In the swimming pool

50 [п’ятдесят]
50 [p”yatdesyat]

В басейні
V baseÿni

It is hot today.	Сьогодні гаряче. S’ohodni haryache.
Shall we go to the swimming pool?	Йдемо в басейн? Ÿdemo v baseÿn?
Do you feel like swimming?	Маєш бажання йти плавати? Mayesh bazhannya ÿty plavaty?
Do you have a towel?	Маєш рушник? Mayesh rushnyk?
Do you have swimming trunks?	Маєш плавки? Mayesh plavky?
Do you have a bathing suit?	Маєш купальник? Mayesh kupal’nyk?
Can you swim?	Чи ти вмієш плавати? Chy ty vmiyesh plavaty?
Can you dive?	Чи ти вмієш пірнати? Chy ty vmiyesh pirnaty?
Can you jump in the water?	Чи ти вмієш стрибати у воду? Chy ty vmiyesh strybaty u vodu?

50 [fifty]

In the swimming pool

50 [п’ятдесят]
50 [p”yatdesyat]

В басейні
V baseÿni

Where is the shower? | Де є душ?
De ye dush?

Where is the changing room? | Де є кабіни для перевдягання?
De ye kabiny dlya perevdyahannya?

Where are the swimming goggles? | Де є окуляри для плавання?
De ye okulyary dlya plavannya?

Is the water deep? | Тут глибоко?
Tut hlyboko?

Is the water clean? | Вода чиста?
Voda chysta?

Is the water warm? | Вода тепла?
Voda tepla?

I am freezing. | Мені холодно.
Meni kholodno.

The water is too cold. | Вода надто холодна.
Voda nadto kholodna.

I am getting out of the water now. | Я йду тепер з води.
YA ÿdu teper z vody.

51 [fifty-one]

51 [п’ятдесят один]
51 [p”yatdesyat odyn]

Running errands

Робити покупки
Robyty pokupky

I want to go to the library.
Я хочу в бібліотеку.
YA khochu v biblioteku.

I want to go to the bookstore.
Я хочу до книжкового магазину.
YA khochu do knyzhkovoho mahazynu.

I want to go to the newspaper stand.
Я хочу до кіоску.
YA khochu do kiosku.

I want to borrow a book.
Я хочу позичити книгу.
YA khochu pozychyty knyhu.

I want to buy a book.
Я хочу купити книгу.
YA khochu kupyty knyhu.

I want to buy a newspaper.
Я хочу купити газету.
YA khochu kupyty hazetu.

I want to go to the library to borrow a book.
Я хочу в бібліотеку, щоб взяти книгу.
YA khochu v biblioteku, shchob vzyaty knyhu.

I want to go to the bookstore to buy a book.
Я хочу до книжкового магазину, щоб купити книгу.
YA khochu do knyzhkovoho mahazynu, shchob kupyty knyhu.

I want to go to the kiosk / newspaper stand to buy a newspaper.
Я хочу до кіоску, щоб купити газету.
YA khochu do kiosku, shchob kupyty hazetu.

51 [fifty-one]

51 [п’ятдесят один]
51 [p”yatdesyat odyn]

Running errands

Робити покупки
Robyty pokupky

I want to go to the optician.	Я хочу піти в оптику. YA khochu pity v optyku.
I want to go to the supermarket.	Я хочу в супермаркет. YA khochu v supermarket.
I want to go to the bakery.	Я хочу сходити в булочну. YA khochu skhodyty v bulochnu.
I want to buy some glasses.	Я хочу купити окуляри. YA khochu kupyty okulyary.
I want to buy fruit and vegetables.	Я хочу купити фрукти і овочі. YA khochu kupyty frukty i ovochi.
I want to buy rolls and bread.	Я хочу купити булочки і хліб. YA khochu kupyty bulochky i khlib.
I want to go to the optician to buy glasses.	Я хочу піти в оптику, щоб купити окуляри. YA khochu pity v optyku, shchob kupyty okulyary.
I want to go to the supermarket to buy fruit and vegetables.	Я хочу в супермаркет, щоб купити фрукти і овочі. YA khochu v supermarket, shchob kupyty frukty i ovochi.
I want to go to the baker to buy rolls and bread.	Я хочу до булочної, щоб купити булочки і хліб. YA khochu do bulochnoï, shchob kupyty bulochky i khlib.

52 [fifty-two]

In the department store

52 [п’ятдесят два]
52 [p”yatdesyat dva]

В магазині
V mahazyni

Shall we go to the department store?	Йдемо в магазин? Ўdemo v mahazyn?
I have to go shopping.	Я повинен / повинна зробити закупи. YA povynen / povynna zrobyty zakupy.
I want to do a lot of shopping.	Я хочу зробити багато закупів. YA khochu zrobyty bahato zakupiv.
Where are the office supplies?	Де є канцелярські товари? De ye kantselyars’ki tovary?
I need envelopes and stationery.	Мені потрібні конверти і поштовий папір. Meni potribni konverty i poshtovyў papir.
I need pens and markers.	Мені потрібні ручки та фломастери. Meni potribni ruchky ta flomastery.
Where is the furniture?	Де є меблі? De ye mebli?
I need a cupboard and a chest of drawers.	Мені потрібні шафа і комод. Meni potribni shafa i komod.
I need a desk and a bookshelf.	Мені потрібні письмовий стіл і полиця. Meni potribni pys’movyў stil i polytsya.

52 [fifty-two]

In the department store

52 [п'ятдесят два]
52 [p"yatdesyat dva]

В магазині
V mahazyni

Where are the toys?	Де є іграшки? De ye ihrashky?
I need a doll and a teddy bear.	Мені потрібні лялька і плюшевий ведмедик. Meni potribni lyal'ka i plyushevyў vedmedyk.
I need a football and a chess board.	Мені потрібні футбольний м'яч і шахи. Meni potribni futbol'nyў m'yach i shakhy.
Where are the tools?	Де є інструменти? De ye instrumenty?
I need a hammer and a pair of pliers.	Мені потрібні молоток і пласкогубці. Meni potribni molotok i plaskohubtsi.
I need a drill and a screwdriver.	Мені потрібні дриль і викрутка. Meni potribni dryl' i vykrutka.
Where is the jewellery / jewelry (am.) department?	Де є прикраси? De ye prykrasy?
I need a chain and a bracelet.	Мені потрібні ланцюжок і браслет. Meni potribni lantsyuzhok i braslet.
I need a ring and earrings.	Мені потрібні перстень і сережки. Meni potribni persten' i serezhky.

53 [fifty-three]

53 [п’ятдесят три]
53 [p”yatdesyat try]

Shops

Магазини
Mahazyny

We’re looking for a sports shop.	Ми шукаємо спортивний магазин. My shukayemo sportyvnyў mahazyn.
We’re looking for a butcher shop.	Ми шукаємо м’ясний магазин. My shukayemo m'yasnyў mahazyn.
We’re looking for a pharmacy / drugstore (am.).	Ми шукаємо аптеку. My shukayemo apteku.
We want to buy a football.	Ми хотіли б купити футбольний м’яч. My khotily b kupyty futbol’nyў m'yach.
We want to buy salami.	Ми хотіли б купити салямі. My khotily b kupyty salyami.
We want to buy medicine.	Ми хотіли б купити ліки. My khotily b kupyty liky.
We’re looking for a sports shop to buy a football.	Ми шукаємо спортивний магазин, щоб купити футбольний м’яч. My shukayemo sportyvnyў mahazyn, shchob kupyty futbol’nyў m'yach.
We’re looking for a butcher shop to buy salami.	Ми шукаємо м’ясний магазин, щоб купити салямі. My shukayemo m'yasnyў mahazyn, shchob kupyty salyami.
We’re looking for a drugstore to buy medicine.	Ми шукаємо аптеку, щоб купити ліки. My shukayemo apteku, shchob kupyty liky.

53 [fifty-three]

53 [п’ятдесят три]
53 [p”yatdesyat try]

Shops

Магазини
Mahazyny

I’m looking for a jeweller / jeweler (am.).	Я шукаю ювелірний магазин. YA shukayu yuvelirnyў mahazyn.
I’m looking for a photo equipment store.	Я шукаю фотомагазин. YA shukayu fotomahazyn.
I’m looking for a confectionery.	Я шукаю кондитерську. YA shukayu kondyters’ku.
I actually plan to buy a ring.	Я маю намір купити перстень. YA mayu namir kupyty persten’.
I actually plan to buy a roll of film.	Я маю намір купити плівку. YA mayu namir kupyty plivku.
I actually plan to buy a cake.	Я маю намір купити торт. YA mayu namir kupyty tort.
I’m looking for a jeweler to buy a ring.	Я шукаю ювелірний магазин, щоб купити перстень. YA shukayu yuvelirnyў mahazyn, shchob kupyty persten’.
I’m looking for a photo shop to buy a roll of film.	Я шукаю фотомагазин, щоб купити плівку. YA shukayu fotomahazyn, shchob kupyty plivku.
I’m looking for a confectionery to buy a cake.	Я шукаю кондитерську, щоб купити торт. YA shukayu kondyters’ku, shchob kupyty tort.

54 [fifty-four]

Shopping

54 [п'ятдесят чотири]
54 [p"yatdesyat chotyry]

Покупки
Pokupky

I want to buy a present.	Я хотів би / хотіла б купити подарунок. YA khotiv by / khotila b kupyty podarunok.
But nothing too expensive.	Але не дуже дорогий. Ale ne duzhe dorohyў.
Maybe a handbag?	Можливо сумку? Mozhlyvo sumku?
Which color would you like?	Якого кольору Ви б хотіли? Yakoho kol'oru Vy b khotily?
Black, brown or white?	Чорного, коричневого чи білого? Chornoho, korychnevoho chy biloho?
A large one or a small one?	Велику чи маленьку? Velyku chy malen'ku?
May I see this one, please?	Чи можу я на цю глянути? Chy mozhu ya na tsyu hlyanuty?
Is it made of leather?	Вона шкіряна? Vona shkiryana?
Or is it made of plastic?	Чи вона зі штучного матеріалу? Chy vona zi shtuchnoho materialu?

54 [fifty-four]

Shopping

54 [п’ятдесят чотири]
54 [p”yatdesyat chotyry]

Покупки
Pokupky

Of leather, of course.	Зі шкіри, звичайно. Zi shkiry, zvychaўno.
This is very good quality.	Це дуже хороша якість. Tse duzhe khorosha yakist’.
And the bag is really very reasonable.	І сумка дійсно зовсім не дорога. I sumka diўsno zovsim ne doroha.
I like it.	Ця мені подобається. Tsya meni podobayet’sya.
I’ll take it.	Я цю візьму. YA tsyu viz’mu.
Can I exchange it if needed?	Чи можу я цю обміняти? Chy mozhu ya tsyu obminyaty?
Of course.	Звичайно. Zvychaўno.
We’ll gift wrap it.	Ми запакуємо її як подарунок. My zapakuyemo ïï yak podarunok.
The cashier is over there.	Каса там. Kasa tam.

55 [fifty-five]

55 [п’ятдесят п’ять]

55 [p”yatdesyat p”yat’]

Working

Робота

Robota

What do you do for a living?

Хто Ви за професією?

Khto Vy za profesiyeyu?

My husband is a doctor.

Мій чоловік – лікар за професією.

Miӳ cholovik – likar za profesiyeyu.

I work as a nurse part-time.

Я працюю медсестрою на пів ставки.

YA pratsyuyu medsestroyu na piv stavky.

We will soon receive our pension.

Скоро ми будемо отримувати пенсію.

Skoro my budemo otrymuvaty pensiyu.

But taxes are high.

Але податки високі.

Ale podatky vysoki.

And health insurance is expensive.

І медстрахування дороге.

I medstrakhuvannya dorohe.

What would you like to become some day?

Ким ти хочеш колись стати?

Kym ty khochesh kolys’ staty?

I would like to become an engineer.

Я хотів би стати інженером.

YA khotiv by staty inzhenerom.

I want to go to college.

Я хочу навчатися в університеті.

YA khochu navchatysya v universyteti.

55 [fifty-five]

55 [п’ятдесят п’ять]
55 [p”yatdesyat p”yat’]

Working

Робота
Robota

I am an intern.	Я практикант. YA praktykant.
I do not earn much.	Я заробляю небагато. YA zaroblyayu nebahato.
I am doing an internship abroad.	Я проходжу практику за кордоном. YA prokhodzhu praktyku za kordonom.
That is my boss.	Це мій керівник. Tse miў kerivnyk.
I have nice colleagues.	Я маю люб’язних колег. YA mayu lyub”yaznykh koleh.
We always go to the cafeteria at noon.	На обід ми завжди ходимо до їдальні. Na obid my zavzhdy khodymo do ïdal'ni.
I am looking for a job.	Я шукаю роботу. YA shukayu robotu.
I have already been unemployed for a year.	Я вже рік безробітний / безробітна. YA vzhe rik bezrobitnyў / bezrobitna.
There are too many unemployed people in this country.	У цій країні є забагато безробітних. U tsiў kraïni ye zabahato bezrobitnykh.

56 [fifty-six]

56 [п’ятдесят шість]
56 [p”yatdesyat shist’]

Feelings

Почуття
Pochuttya

to feel like / want to	Мати бажання Maty bazhannya
We feel like. / We want to.	Ми маємо бажання. My mayemo bazhannya.
We don’t feel like. / We do’t want to.	Ми не маємо бажання. My ne mayemo bazhannya.
to be afraid	Боятися. Boyatysya.
I’m afraid.	Я боюся. YA boyusya.
I am not afraid.	Я не боюся. YA ne boyusya.
to have time	Мати час Maty chas
He has time.	Він має час. Vin maye chas.
He has no time.	Він не має часу. Vin ne maye chasu.

56 [fifty-six]

56 [п'ятдесят шість]
56 [p"yatdesyat shist']

Feelings

Почуття
Pochuttya

to be bored	Нудьгувати Nud'huvaty
She is bored.	Вона нудьгує. Vona nud'huye.
She is not bored.	Вона не нудьгує. Vona ne nud'huye.
to be hungry	Бути голодним Buty holodnym
Are you hungry?	Ви голодні? Vy holodni?
Aren't you hungry?	Ви не голодні? Vy ne holodni?
to be thirsty	Мати спрагу Maty sprahu
They are thirsty.	Вони мають спрагу. Vony mayut' sprahu.
They are not thirsty.	Вони не мають спраги. Vony ne mayut' sprahy.

57 [fifty-seven]

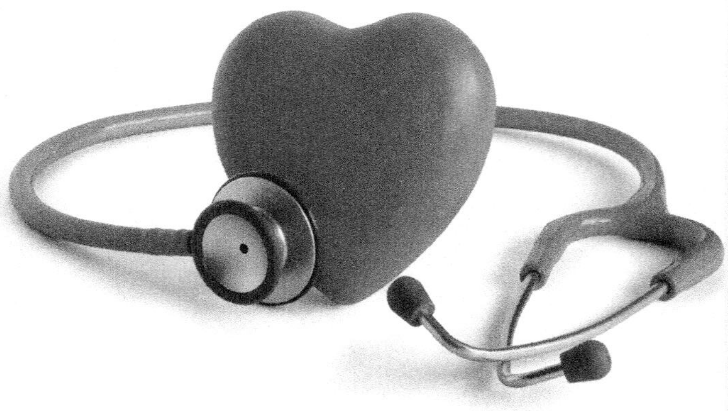

57 [п’ятдесят сім]
57 [p”yatdesyat sim]

At the doctor

У лікаря
U likarya

I have a doctor’s appointment.	У мене візит до лікаря. U mene vizyt do likarya.
I have the appointment at ten o’clock.	У мене візит на десяту годину. U mene vizyt na desyatu hodynu.
What is your name?	Як Вас звати? Yak Vas zvaty?
Please take a seat in the waiting room.	Займіть, будь-ласка, місце в приймальні. Zaўmit’, bud’-laska, mistse v pryўmal’ni.
The doctor is on his way.	Лікар зараз прийде. Likar zaraz pryўde.
What insurance company do you belong to?	Де Ви застраховані? De Vy zastrakhovani?
What can I do for you?	Що я можу для Вас зробити? Shcho ya mozhu dlya Vas zrobyty?
Do you have any pain?	У вас щось болить? U vas shchos’ bolyt’?
Where does it hurt?	Де болить? De bolyt’?

57 [fifty-seven]

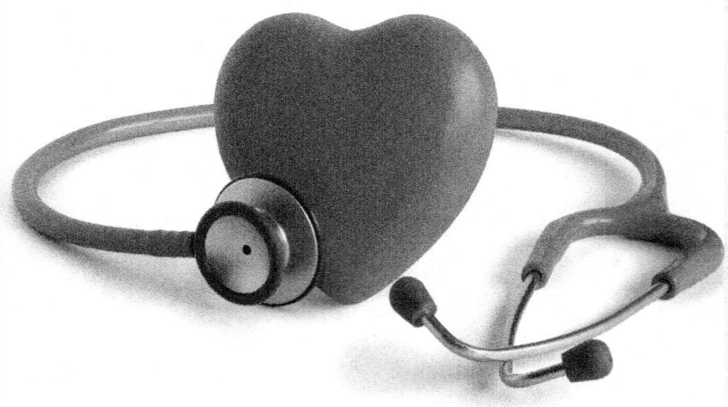

57 [п'ятдесят сім]
57 [p"yatdesyat sim]

At the doctor

У лікаря
U likarya

I always have back pain.	Я маю завжди болі в спині. YA mayu zavzhdy boli v spyni.
I often have headaches.	Я маю часто біль голови. YA mayu chasto bil' holovy.
I sometimes have stomach aches.	Я маю іноді болі в животі. YA mayu inodi boli v zhyvoti.
Remove your top!	Роздягніться, будь-ласка, до пояса! Rozdyahnit'sya, bud'-laska, do poyasa!
Lie down on the examining table.	Приляжте, будь-ласка, на кушетку! Prylyazhte, bud'-laska, na kushetku!
Your blood pressure is okay.	Тиск в порядку. Tysk v poryadku.
I will give you an injection.	Я зроблю Вам укол. YA zroblyu Vam ukol.
I will give you some pills.	Я дам Вам таблетки. YA dam Vam tabletky.
I am giving you a prescription for the pharmacy.	Я дам Вам рецепт для аптеки. YA dam Vam retsept dlya apteky.

58 [fifty-eight]

Parts of the body

58 [п'ятдесят вісім]
58 [p"yatdesyat visim]

Частини тіла
Chastyny tila

I am drawing a man.
Я малюю чоловіка.
YA malyuyu cholovika.

First the head.
Спочатку голову.
Spochatku holovu.

The man is wearing a hat.
Чоловік носить капелюх.
Cholovik nosyt' kapelyukh.

One cannot see the hair.
Волосся не видно.
Volossya ne vydno.

One cannot see the ears either.
Вух не видно також.
Vukh ne vydno takozh.

One cannot see his back either.
Спини також не видно.
Spyny takozh ne vydno.

I am drawing the eyes and the mouth.
Я малюю очі і рот.
YA malyuyu ochi i rot.

The man is dancing and laughing.
Чоловік танцює і сміється.
Cholovik tantsyuye i smiyet'sya.

The man has a long nose.
Чоловік має довгий ніс.
Cholovik maye dovhyў nis.

58 [fifty-eight]

Parts of the body

58 [п’ятдесят вісім]
58 [p”yatdesyat visim]

Частини тіла
Chastyny tila

He is carrying a cane in his hands.	Він носить у руках палицю. Vin nosyt’ u rukakh palytsyu.
He is also wearing a scarf around his neck.	Він також має на шиї кашне. Vin takozh maye na shyï kashne.
It is winter and it is cold.	Це зима і холодно. Tse zyma i kholodno.
The arms are athletic.	Руки сильні. Ruky syl’ni.
The legs are also athletic.	Ноги також сильні. Nohy takozh syl’ni.
The man is made of snow.	Чоловік зі снігу. Cholovik zi snihu.
He is neither wearing pants nor a coat.	Він не носить штанів і пальта. Vin ne nosyt’ shtaniv i pal’ta.
But the man is not freezing.	Але чоловік не мерзне. Ale cholovik ne merzne.
He is a snowman.	Він – сніговик. Vin – snihovyk.

59 [fifty-nine]

At the post office

59 [п'ятдесят дев'ять]

59 [p"yatdesyat dev"yat']

На пошті

Na poshti

Where is the nearest post office?	Де найближча пошта? De nay̆blyzhcha poshta?
Is the post office far from here?	Чи далеко до найближчої пошти? Chy daleko do nay̆blyzhchoï poshty?
Where is the nearest mail box?	Де найближча поштова скринька? De nay̆blyzhcha poshtova skryn'ka?
I need a couple of stamps.	Мені потрібно кілька поштових марок. Meni potribno kil'ka poshtovykh marok.
For a card and a letter.	Для листівки і листа. Dlya lystivky i lysta.
How much is the postage to America?	Скільки коштує поштовий збір в Америку? Skil'ky koshtuye poshtovyy̆ zbir v Ameryku?
How heavy is the package?	Скільки важить пакунок? Skil'ky vazhyt' pakunok?
Can I send it by air mail?	Чи можу я послати це авіапоштою? Chy mozhu ya poslaty tse aviaposhtoyu?
How long will it take to get there?	Як довго він ітиме? Yak dovho vin ityme?

59 [fifty-nine]

59 [п’ятдесят дев’ять]
59 [p”yatdesyat dev”yat’]

At the post office

На пошті
Na poshti

Where can I make a call?
Звідки я можу зателефонувати?
Zvidky ya mozhu zatelefonuvaty?

Where is the nearest telephone booth?
Де найближчий телефонний автомат?
De naÿblyzhchyÿ telefonnyÿ avtomat?

Do you have calling cards?
Ви маєте телефонні картки?
Vy mayete telefonni kartky?

Do you have a telephone directory?
Ви маєте телефонний довідник?
Vy mayete telefonnyÿ dovidnyk?

Do you know the area code for Austria?
Ви знаєте код Австрії?
Vy znayete kod Avstriï?

One moment, I’ll look it up.
Хвилинку, я подивлюся.
Khvylynku, ya podyvlyusya.

The line is always busy.
Лінія завжди зайнята.
Liniya zavzhdy zaÿnyata.

Which number did you dial?
Який номер ви набрали?
Yakyÿ nomer vy nabraly?

You have to dial a zero first!
Ви повинні набрати спочатку нуль!
Vy povynni nabraty spochatku nul’!

60 [sixty]

60 [шістдесят]
60 [shistdesyat]

At the bank

В банку
V banku

I would like to open an account.
Я хотів би / хотіла б відкрити рахунок.
YA khotiv by / khotila b vidkryty rakhunok.

Here is my passport.
Ось мій паспорт.
Os' miy̆ pasport.

And here is my address.
А ось моя адреса.
A os' moya adresa.

I want to deposit money in my account.
Я хотів би / хотіла б покласти гроші на мій рахунок.
YA khotiv by / khotila b poklasty hroshi na miy̆ rakhunok.

I want to withdraw money from my account.
Я хотів би / хотіла б зняти гроші з мого рахунку.
YA khotiv by / khotila b znyaty hroshi z moho rakhunku.

I want to pick up the bank statements.
Я хотів би / хотіла б взяти виписки з рахунку.
YA khotiv by / khotila b vzyaty vypysky z rakhunku.

I want to cash a traveller's cheque / traveler's check (am.).
Я хотів би / хотіла б отримати гроші по чеку.
YA khotiv by / khotila b otrymaty hroshi po cheku.

What are the fees?
Яка сума комісії?
Yaka suma komisiï?

Where should I sign?
Де я повинен / повинна підписати?
De ya povynen / povynna pidpysaty?

60 [sixty]

60 [шістдесят]
60 [shistdesyat]

At the bank

В банку
V banku

I'm expecting a transfer from Germany.	Я чекаю на грошовий переказ з Німеччини. YA chekayu na hroshovyy̆ perekaz z Nimechchyny.
Here is my account number.	Тут є номер мого рахунку. Tut ye nomer moho rakhunku.
Has the money arrived?	Чи прибули гроші? Chy prybuly hroshi?
I want to change money.	Я хотів би / хотіла б поміняти ці гроші. YA khotiv by / khotila b pominyaty tsi hroshi.
I need US-Dollars.	Мені потрібні долари США. Meni potribni dolary SSHA.
Could you please give me small notes / bills (am.)?	Дайте мені, будь-ласка, дрібні купюри. Day̆te meni, bud'-laska, dribni kupyury.
Is there a cashpoint / an ATM (am.)?	Тут є банкомат? Tut ye bankomat?
How much money can one withdraw?	Скільки грошей можна зняти? Skil'ky hroshey̆ mozhna znyaty?
Which credit cards can one use?	Які кредитні картки можна використовувати? Yaki kredytni kartky mozhna vykorystovuvaty?

61 [sixty-one]

Ordinal numbers

61 [шістдесят один]

61 [shistdesyat odyn]

Порядкові числа

Poryadkovi chysla

The first month is January.

Перший місяць – січень.

Pershyў misyats' – sichen'.

The second month is February.

Другий місяць – лютий.

Druhyў misyats' – lyutyў.

The third month is March.

Третій місяць – березень.

Tretiў misyats' – berezen'.

The fourth month is April.

Четвертий місяць – квітень.

Chetvertyў misyats' – kviten'.

The fifth month is May.

П'ятий місяць – травень.

P"yatyў misyats' – traven'.

The sixth month is June.

Шостий місяць – червень.

Shostyў misyats' – cherven'.

Six months make half a year.

Шість місяців – це півроку.

Shist' misyatsiv – tse pivroku.

January, February, March,

Січень, лютий, березень,

Sichen', lyutyў, berezen',

April, May and June.

квітень, травень і червень.

kviten', traven' i cherven'.

61 [sixty-one]

61 [шістдесят один]
61 [shistdesyat odyn]

Ordinal numbers

Порядкові числа
Poryadkovi chysla

The seventh month is July.
Сьомий місяць – липень.
S’omyў misyats’ – lypen’.

The eighth month is August.
Восьмий місяць – серпень.
Vos’myў misyats’ – serpen’.

The ninth month is September.
Дев’ятий місяць – вересень.
Dev'yatyў misyats’ – veresen’.

The tenth month is October.
Десятий місяць – жовтень.
Desyatyў misyats’ – zhovten’.

The eleventh month is November.
Одинадцятий місяць – листопад.
Odynadtsyatyў misyats’ – lystopad.

The twelfth month is December.
Дванадцятий місяць – грудень.
Dvanadtsyatyў misyats’ – hruden’.

Twelve months make a year.
Дванадцять місяців – це рік.
Dvanadtsyat’ misyatsiv – tse rik.

July, August, September,
Липень, серпень, вересень,
Lypen’, serpen’, veresen’,

October, November and December.
жовтень, листопад і грудень.
zhovten’, lystopad i hruden’.

62 [sixty-two]

Asking questions 1

62 [шістдесят два]
62 [shistdesyat dva]

Ставити запитання 1

Stavyty zapytannya 1

to learn	Вчитися Vchytysya
Do the students learn a lot?	Учні багато вчаться? Uchni bahato vchat'sya?
No, they learn a little.	Ні, вони вчаться мало. Ni, vony vchat'sya malo.
to ask	Запитувати Zapytuvaty
Do you often ask the teacher questions?	Ви часто запитуєте вчителя? Vy chasto zapytuyete vchytelya?
No, I don't ask him questions often.	Ні, я не часто його запитую. Ni, ya ne chasto ŷoho zapytuyu.
to reply	Відповідати Vidpovidaty
Please reply.	Відповідайте, будь-ласка. Vidpovidaŷte, bud'-laska.
I reply.	Я відповідаю. YA vidpovidayu.

62 [sixty-two]

Asking questions 1

62 [шістдесят два]
62 [shistdesyat dva]

Ставити запитання 1
Stavyty zapytannya 1

to work — Працювати
Pratsyuvaty

Is he working right now? — Він зараз працює?
Vin zaraz pratsyuye?

Yes, he is working right now. — Так, він зараз працює.
Tak, vin zaraz pratsyuye.

to come — Приходити
Prykhodyty

Are you coming? — Ви йдете?
Vy ўdete?

Yes, we are coming soon. — Так, ми зараз прийдемо.
Tak, my zaraz pryўdemo.

to live — Жити
Zhyty

Do you live in Berlin? — Ви живете в Берліні?
Vy zhyvete v Berlini?

Yes, I live in Berlin. — Так, я живу в Берліні.
Tak, ya zhyvu v Berlini.

63 [sixty-three]

Asking questions 2

63 [шістдесят три]
63 [shistdesyat try]

Ставити запитання 2
Stavyty zapytannya 2

I have a hobby.	Я маю хобі. YA mayu khobi.
I play tennis.	Я граю в теніс. YA hrayu v tenis.
Where is the tennis court?	Де є тенісний корт? De ye tenisnyy̆ kort?
Do you have a hobby?	Чи маєш ти хобі? Chy mayesh ty khobi?
I play football / soccer (am.).	Я граю у футбол. YA hrayu u futbol.
Where is the football / soccer (am.) field?	Де є футбольний майданчик? De ye futbol'nyy̆ may̆danchyk?
My arm hurts.	В мене болить рам'я. V mene bolyt' ram"ya.
My foot and hand also hurt.	Моя нога і моя рука також болять. Moya noha i moya ruka takozh bolyat'.
Is there a doctor?	Де є лікар? De ye likar?

63 [sixty-three]

Asking questions 2

63 [шістдесят три]
63 [shistdesyat try]

Ставити запитання 2
Stavyty zapytannya 2

I have a car / an automobile.	Я маю автомобіль. YA mayu avtomobil'.
I also have a motorcycle.	Я маю також мотоцикл. YA mayu takozh mototsykl.
Where could I park?	Де є місце для парковки? De ye mistse dlya parkovky?
I have a sweater.	Я маю светр. YA mayu svetr.
I also have a jacket and a pair of jeans.	Я маю також куртку і джинси. YA mayu takozh kurtku i dzhynsy.
Where is the washing machine?	Де є пральна машина? De ye pral'na mashyna?
I have a plate.	Я маю тарілку. YA mayu tarilku.
I have a knife, a fork and a spoon.	Я маю ніж, виделку і ложку. YA mayu nizh, vydelku i lozhku.
Where is the salt and pepper?	Де є сіль і перець? De ye sil' i perets'?

64 [sixty-four]

64 [шістдесят чотири]
64 [shistdesyat chotyry]

Negation 1

заперечення 1
zaperechennya 1

I don't understand the word.	Я не розумію цього слова. YA ne rozumiyu ts'oho slova.
I don't understand the sentence.	Я не розумію цього речення. YA ne rozumiyu ts'oho rechennya.
I don't understand the meaning.	Я не розумію, що це означає. YA ne rozumiyu, shcho tse oznachaye.
the teacher	Вчитель Vchytel'
Do you understand the teacher?	Ви розумієте вчителя? Vy rozumiyete vchytelya?
Yes, I understand him well.	Так, я його добре розумію. Tak, ya ŷoho dobre rozumiyu.
the teacher	Вчителька Vchytel'ka
Do you understand the teacher?	Ви розумієте вчительку? Vy rozumiyete vchytel'ku?
Yes, I understand her well.	Так, я її добре розумію. Tak, ya ïi dobre rozumiyu.

64 [sixty-four]

64 [шістдесят чотири]

64 [shistdesyat chotyry]

Negation 1

заперечення 1

zaperechennya 1

the people	Люди Lyudy
Do you understand the people?	Ви розумієте людей? Vy rozumiyete lyudeў?
No, I don't understand them so well.	Ні, я їх не дуже добре розумію. Ni, ya ïkh ne duzhe dobre rozumiyu.
the girlfriend	Подруга Podruha
Do you have a girlfriend?	Ви маєте подругу? Vy mayete podruhu?
Yes, I do.	Так, маю. Tak, mayu.
the daughter	Дочка Dochka
Do you have a daughter?	Ви маєте дочку? Vy mayete dochku?
No, I don't.	Ні, не маю. Ni, ne mayu.

65 [sixty-five]

Negation 2

65 [шістдесят п’ять]
65 [shistdesyat p”yat’]

Заперечення 2

Zaperechennya 2

Is the ring expensive?	Перстень дорогий? Persten’ dorohyў?
No, it costs only one hundred Euros.	Ні, він коштує тільки сто євро. Ni, vin koshtuye til’ky sto yevro.
But I have only fifty.	Але я маю тільки п’ятдесят. Ale ya mayu til’ky p'yatdesyat.
Are you finished?	Ти вже готовий / готова? Ty vzhe hotovyў / hotova?
No, not yet.	Ні, ще ні. Ni, shche ni.
But I’ll be finished soon.	Але скоро буду готовий / готова. Ale skoro budu hotovyў / hotova.
Do you want some more soup?	Хочеш ще супу? Khochesh shche supu?
No, I don’t want anymore.	Ні, я більше не хочу. Ni, ya bil’she ne khochu.
But another ice cream.	Але ще одне морозиво. Ale shche odne morozyvo.

65 [sixty-five]

Negation 2

65 [шістдесят п’ять]
65 [shistdesyat p”yat’]

Заперечення 2
Zaperechennya 2

Have you lived here long? — Ти довго вже тут живеш?
Ty dovho vzhe tut zhyvesh?

No, only for a month. — Ні, тільки місяць.
Ni, til’ky misyats’.

But I already know a lot of people. — Але я знаю вже багато людей.
Ale ya znayu vzhe bahato lyudeў.

Are you driving home tomorrow? — Їдеш завтра додому?
Ïdesh zavtra dodomu?

No, only on the weekend. — Ні, тільки у вихідні.
Ni, til’ky u vykhidni.

But I will be back on Sunday. — Але я повертаюся вже у неділю.
Ale ya povertayusya vzhe u nedilyu.

Is your daughter an adult? — Твоя дочка вже доросла?
Tvoya dochka vzhe dorosla?

No, she is only seventeen. — Ні, їй тільки сімнадцять.
Ni, їў til’ky simnadtsyat’.

But she already has a boyfriend. — Але вона вже має хлопця.
Ale vona vzhe maye khloptsya.

66 [sixty-six]

Possessive pronouns 1

66 [шістдесят шість]
66 [shistdesyat shist’]

Присвійні займенники 1
Prysviy̆ni zay̆mennyky 1

I – my	я – мій ya – miy̆
I can’t find my key.	Я не можу знайти мого ключа. YA ne mozhu znay̆ty moho klyucha.
I can’t find my ticket.	Я не можу знайти мого квитка. YA ne mozhu znay̆ty moho kvytka.
you – your	ти – твій ty – tviy̆
Have you found your key?	Ти знайшов твій ключ? Ty znay̆shov tviy̆ klyuch?
Have you found your ticket?	Ти знайшов твій проїзний квиток? Ty znay̆shov tviy̆ proïznyy̆ kvytok?
he – his	він – його vin – y̆oho
Do you know where his key is?	Знаєш, де його ключ? Znayesh, de y̆oho klyuch?
Do you know where his ticket is?	Знаєш, де його проїзний квиток? Znayesh, de y̆oho proïznyy̆ kvytok?

66 [sixty-six]

66 [шістдесят шість]
66 [shistdesyat shist’]

Possessive pronouns 1

Присвійні займенники 1
Prysviÿni zaÿmennyky 1

she – her

вона – її
vona – її

Her money is gone.

Її грошей немає.
Її hrosheÿ nemaye.

And her credit card is also gone.

І її кредитної картки також немає.
I її kredytnoї kartky takozh nemaye.

we – our

ми – наш
my – nash

Our grandfather is ill.

Наш дідусь хворий.
Nash didus’ khvoryÿ.

Our grandmother is healthy.

Наша бабуся здорова.
Nasha babusya zdorova.

you – your

ви – ваш
vy – vash

Children, where is your father?

Діти, де ваш тато?
Dity, de vash tato?

Children, where is your mother?

Діти, де ваша мама?
Dity, de vasha mama?

67 [sixty-seven]

67 [шістдесят сім]
67 [shistdesyat sim]

Possessive pronouns 2

Присвійні займенники 2
Prysviy̆ni zay̆mennyky 2

the glasses	Окуляри Okulyary
He has forgotten his glasses.	Він забув свої окуляри. Vin zabuv svoï okulyary.
Where has he left his glasses?	Де ж його окуляри? De zh y̆oho okulyary?
the clock	Годинник Hodynnyk
His clock isn't working.	Його годинник попсутий. Y̆oho hodynnyk popsutyy̆.
The clock hangs on the wall.	Годинник висить на стіні. Hodynnyk vysyt' na stini.
the passport	Паспорт Pasport
He has lost his passport.	Він загубив свій паспорт. Vin zahubyv sviy̆ pasport.
Where is his passport then?	Де ж його паспорт? De zh y̆oho pasport?

67 [sixty-seven]

67 [шістдесят сім]
67 [shistdesyat sim]

Possessive pronouns 2

Присвійні займенники 2
Prysviÿni zaÿmennyky 2

they – their	вони – їх vony – ïkh
The children cannot find their parents.	Діти не можуть знайти своїх батьків. Dity ne mozhut' znaÿty svoïkh bat'kiv.
Here come their parents!	Але ж ось йдуть їх батьки! Ale zh os' ÿdut' ïkh bat'ky!
you – your	Ви – Ваш Vy – Vash
How was your trip, Mr. Miller?	Як ваша подорож, пане Мюллер? Yak vasha podorozh, pane Myuller?
Where is your wife, Mr. Miller?	Де ваша дружина, пане Мюллер? De vasha druzhyna, pane Myuller?
you – your	Ви – ваша Vy – vasha
How was your trip, Mrs. Smith?	Як ваша подорож пані Шмідт? Yak vasha podorozh pani Shmidt?
Where is your husband, Mrs. Smith?	Де Ваш чоловік, пані Шмідт? De Vash cholovik, pani Shmidt?

68 [sixty-eight]

big – small

68 [шістдесят вісім]
68 [shistdesyat visim]

Великий – малий
Velykyў – malyў

big and small

Великий і малий
Velykyў i malyў

The elephant is big.

Слон великий.
Slon velykyў.

The mouse is small.

Миша маленька.
Mysha malen’ka.

dark and bright

Темний і ясний
Temnyў i yasnyў

The night is dark.

Ніч темна.
Nich temna.

The day is bright.

День ясний.
Den’ yasnyў.

old and young

старий і молодий
staryў i molodyў

Our grandfather is very old.

Наш дід дуже старий.
Nash did duzhe staryў.

70 years ago he was still young.

70 років тому він був ще молодий.
70 rokiv tomu vin buv shche molodyў.

68 [sixty-eight]

big – small

68 [шістдесят вісім]
68 [shistdesyat visim]

Великий – малий
Velykyў – malyў

beautiful and ugly
гарний і огидний
harnyў i ohydnyў

The butterfly is beautiful.
Метелик гарний.
Metelyk harnyў.

The spider is ugly.
Павук огидний.
Pavuk ohydnyў.

fat and thin
товстий і худий
tovstyў i khudyў

A woman who weighs a hundred kilos is fat.
Жінка вагою 100 кілограм – товста.
Zhinka vahoyu 100 kilohram – tovsta.

A man who weighs fifty kilos is thin.
Чоловік вагою 50 кілограм – худий.
Cholovik vahoyu 50 kilohram – khudyў.

expensive and cheap
Дорогий і дешевий
Dorohyў i deshevyў

The car is expensive.
Автомобіль дорогий.
Avtomobil' dorohyў.

The newspaper is cheap.
Газета дешева.
Hazeta desheva.

69 [sixty-nine]

to need – to want to

69 [шістдесят дев’ять]
69 [shistdesyat dev"yat']

потребувати – хотіти
potrebuvaty – khotity

I need a bed.

I want to sleep.

Is there a bed here?

Мені потрібне ліжко.
Meni potribne lizhko.
Я хочу спати.
YA khochu spaty.
Тут є ліжко?
Tut ye lizhko?

I need a lamp.

I want to read.

Is there a lamp here?

Мені потрібна лампа.
Meni potribna lampa.
Я хочу читати.
YA khochu chytaty.
Чи є тут лампа?
Chy ye tut lampa?

I need a telephone.

I want to make a call.

Is there a telephone here?

Мені потрібен телефон.
Meni potriben telefon.
Я хочу зателефонувати.
YA khochu zatelefonuvaty.
Тут є телефон?
Tut ye telefon?

69 [sixty-nine]

to need – to want to

69 [шістдесят дев’ять]
69 [shistdesyat dev"yat']

потребувати – хотіти
potrebuvaty – khotity

I need a camera.	Мені потрібний фотоапарат. Meni potribnyў fotoaparat.
I want to take photographs.	Я хочу фотографувати. YA khochu fotohrafuvaty.
Is there a camera here?	Тут є фотоапарат? Tut ye fotoaparat?
I need a computer.	Мені потрібен комп’ютер. Meni potriben komp"yuter.
I want to send an email.	Я хочу послати повідомлення електронною поштою. YA khochu poslaty povidomlennya elektronnoyu poshtoyu.
Is there a computer here?	Чи є тут комп’ютер? Chy ye tut komp"yuter?
I need a pen.	Мені потрібна кулькова ручка. Meni potribna kul'kova ruchka.
I want to write something.	Я хочу дещо написати. YA khochu deshcho napysaty.
Is there a sheet of paper and a pen here?	Тут є аркуш паперу і кулькова ручка? Tut ye arkush paperu i kul'kova ruchka?

70 [seventy]

to like something

70 [сімдесят]
70 [simdesyat]

Хотіти що-небудь
Khotity shcho-nebud'

Would you like to smoke?	Хочете курити? Khochete kuryty?
Would you like to dance?	Хочете танцювати? Khochete tantsyuvaty?
Would you like to go for a walk?	Хочете йти гуляти? Khochete ўty hulyaty?
I would like to smoke.	Я хочу курити. YA khochu kuryty.
Would you like a cigarette?	Ти хотів би цигарку? Ty khotiv by tsyharku?
He wants a light.	Він хотів би вогню. Vin khotiv by vohnyu.
I want to drink something.	Я хочу пити. YA khochu pyty.
I want to eat something.	Я хочу їсти. YA khochu ïsty.
I want to relax a little.	Я хочу відпочити. YA khochu vidpochyty.

70 [seventy]

to like something

70 [сімдесят]
70 [simdesyat]

Хотіти що-небудь
Khotity shcho-nebud'

I want to ask you something.	Я хочу Вас дещо запитати. YA khochu Vas deshcho zapytaty.
I want to ask you for something.	Я хочу Вас дещо попросити. YA khochu Vas deshcho poprosyty.
I want to treat you to something.	Я хочу Вас кудись запросити. YA khochu Vas kudys' zaprosyty.
What would you like?	Що Ви хочете випити? Shcho Vy khochete vypyty?
Would you like a coffee?	Чи хотіли б Ви кави? Chy khotily b Vy kavy?
Or do you prefer a tea?	Чи хотіли б Ви краще чаю? Chy khotily b Vy krashche chayu?
We want to drive home.	Ми хотіли б поїхати додому. My khotily b poïkhaty dodomu.
Do you want a taxi?	Чи хотіли б ви таксі? Chy khotily b vy taksi?
They want to make a call.	Вони хочуть зателефонувати. Vony khochut' zatelefonuvaty.

71 [seventy-one]

71 [сімдесят один]
71 [simdesyat odyn]

to want something

Щось хотіти
Shchos' khotity

What do you want to do?
Що ви хочете?
Shcho vy khochete?

Do you want to play football / soccer (am.)?
Хочете грати у футбол?
Khochete hraty u futbol?

Do you want to visit friends?
Чи хочете ви відвідати друзів?
Chy khochete vy vidvidaty druziv?

to want
Хотіти
Khotity

I don’t want to arrive late.
Я не хочу прийти пізно.
YA ne khochu pryÿty pizno.

I don’t want to go there.
Я не хочу туди йти.
YA ne khochu tudy ÿty.

I want to go home.
Я хочу йти додому.
YA khochu ÿty dodomu.

I want to stay at home.
Я хочу залишитися вдома.
YA khochu zalyshytysya vdoma.

I want to be alone.
Я хочу бути сам / сама.
YA khochu buty sam / sama.

71 [seventy-one]

to want something

71 [сімдесят один]
71 [simdesyat odyn]

Щось хотіти
Shchos' khotity

Do you want to stay here?	Чи хочеш ти залишитися тут? Chy khochesh ty zalyshytysya tut?
Do you want to eat here?	Хочеш тут їсти? Khochesh tut ïsty?
Do you want to sleep here?	Хочеш тут спати? Khochesh tut spaty?
Do you want to leave tomorrow?	Хочете від'їжджати завтра? Khochete vid'ïzhdzhaty zavtra?
Do you want to stay till tomorrow?	Чи хочете Ви залишитися до завтра? Chy khochete Vy zalyshytysya do zavtra?
Do you want to pay the bill only tomorrow?	Чи хочете Ви заплатити тільки завтра? Chy khochete Vy zaplatyty til'ky zavtra?
Do you want to go to the disco?	Чи хочете ви на дискотеку? Chy khochete vy na dyskoteku?
Do you want to go to the cinema?	Чи хочете ви у кіно? Chy khochete vy u kino?
Do you want to go to a café?	Чи хочете ви у кафе? Chy khochete vy u kafe?

72 [seventy-two]

to have to do something / must

72 [сімдесят два]
72 [simdesyat dva]

Щось мусити
Shchos' musyty

must
Мусити
Musyty

I must post the letter.
Я мушу відправити лист.
YA mushu vidpravyty lyst.

I must pay the hotel.
Я мушу заплатити за готель.
YA mushu zaplatyty za hotel'.

You must get up early.
Ти мусиш встати рано.
Ty musysh vstaty rano.

You must work a lot.
Ти мусиш багато працювати.
Ty musysh bahato pratsyuvaty.

You must be punctual.
Ти мусиш бути пунктуальним.
Ty musysh buty punktual'nym.

He must fuel / get petrol / get gas (am.).
Він мусить заправитися.
Vin musyt' zapravytysya.

He must repair the car.
Він мусить ремонтувати автомобіль.
Vin musyt' remontuvaty avtomobil'.

He must wash the car.
Він мусить мити автомобіль.
Vin musyt' myty avtomobil'.

72 [seventy-two]

to have to do something / must

72 [сімдесят два]
72 [simdesyat dva]

Щось мусити
Shchos' musyty

She must shop.
Вона мусить робити закупи.
Vona musyt' robyty zakupy.

She must clean the apartment.
Вона мусить прибрати квартиру.
Vona musyt' prybraty kvartyru.

She must wash the clothes.
Вона мусить прати білизну.
Vona musyt' praty bilyznu.

We must go to school at once.
Ми мусимо негайно йти до школи.
My musymo nehaŷno ŷty do shkoly.

We must go to work at once.
Ми мусимо негайно йти на роботу.
My musymo nehaŷno ŷty na robotu.

We must go to the doctor at once.
Ми мусимо негайно йти до лікаря.
My musymo nehaŷno ŷty do likarya.

You must wait for the bus.
Ви мусите чекати на автобус.
Vy musyte chekaty na avtobus.

You must wait for the train.
Ви мусите чекати на поїзд.
Vy musyte chekaty na poïzd.

You must wait for the taxi.
Ви мусите чекати на таксі.
Vy musyte chekaty na taksi.

73 [seventy-three]

to be allowed to

73 [сімдесят три]
73 [simdesyat try]

Щось могти (мати дозвіл)
Shchos' mohty (maty dozvil)

Are you already allowed to drive?	Тобі можна вже водити автомобіль? Tobi mozhna vzhe vodyty avtomobil'?
Are you already allowed to drink alcohol?	Тобі можна вже пити алкоголь? Tobi mozhna vzhe pyty alkohol'?
Are you already allowed to travel abroad alone?	Тобі можна вже їздити самому за кордон? Tobi mozhna vzhe ïzdyty samomu za kordon?
may / to be allowed	Могти Mohty
May we smoke here?	Ми можемо тут курити? My mozhemo tut kuryty?
Is smoking allowed here?	Можна тут курити? Mozhna tut kuryty?
May one pay by credit card?	Можна розрахуватися кредитною карткою? Mozhna rozrakhuvatysya kredytnoyu kartkoyu?
May one pay by cheque / check (am.)?	Можна розрахуватися чеком? Mozhna rozrakhuvatysya chekom?
May one only pay in cash?	Можна заплатити готівкою? Mozhna zaplatyty hotivkoyu?

73 [seventy-three]

to be allowed to

73 [сімдесят три]
73 [simdesyat try]

Щось могти (мати дозвіл)
Shchos' mohty (maty dozvil)

May I just make a call? — Можу я зателефонувати?
Mozhu ya zatelefonuvaty?

May I just ask something? — Можу я запитати?
Mozhu ya zapytaty?

May I just say something? — Можу я щось сказати?
Mozhu ya shchos' skazaty?

He is not allowed to sleep in the park. — Йому не можна спати в парку.
Ÿomu ne mozhna spaty v parku.

He is not allowed to sleep in the car. — Йому не можна спати в автомобілі.
Ÿomu ne mozhna spaty v avtomobili.

He is not allowed to sleep at the train station. — Йому не можна спати на вокзалі.
Ÿomu ne mozhna spaty na vokzali.

May we take a seat? — Можна нам присісти?
Mozhna nam prysisty?

May we have the menu? — Можна нам меню?
Mozhna nam menyu?

May we pay separately? — Чи можемо ми заплатити окремо?
Chy mozhemo my zaplatyty okremo?

74 [seventy-four]

74 [сімдесят чотири]
74 [simdesyat chotyry]

asking for something

Щось просити
Shchos' prosyty

Can you cut my hair?
Можете мене постригти?
Mozhete mene postryhty?

Not too short, please.
Не дуже коротко, будь-ласка.
Ne duzhe korotko, bud'-laska.

A bit shorter, please.
Дещо коротше, будь-ласка.
Deshcho korotshe, bud'-laska.

Can you develop the pictures?
Можете проявити фотографії?
Mozhete proyavyty fotohrafiï?

The pictures are on the CD.
Фотографії – на диску.
Fotohrafiï – na dysku.

The pictures are in the camera.
Фотографії – у фотоапараті.
Fotohrafiï – u fotoaparati.

Can you fix the clock?
Чи можете Ви відремонтувати годинник?
Chy mozhete Vy vidremontuvaty hodynnyk?

The glass is broken.
Скло розбите.
Sklo rozbyte.

The battery is dead / empty.
Батарея розряджена.
Batareya rozryadzhena.

74 [seventy-four]

asking for something

74 [сімдесят чотири]
74 [simdesyat chotyry]

Щось просити
Shchos' prosyty

Can you iron the shirt?

Чи можете попрасувати сорочку?
Chy mozhete poprasuvaty sorochku?

Can you clean the pants / trousers?

Чи можете почистити штани?
Chy mozhete pochystyty shtany?

Can you fix the shoes?

Чи можете відремонтувати черевики?
Chy mozhete vidremontuvaty cherevyky?

Do you have a light?

Чи можете Ви дати мені запальничку?
Chy mozhete Vy daty meni zapal'nychku?

Do you have a match or a lighter?

Чи маєте Ви сірники або запальничку?
Chy mayete Vy sirnyky abo zapal'nychku?

Do you have an ashtray?

Чи маєте Ви попільничку?
Chy mayete Vy popil'nychku?

Do you smoke cigars?

Чи палите Ви сигари?
Chy palyte Vy syhary?

Do you smoke cigarettes?

Чи палите Ви сигарети?
Chy palyte Vy syharety?

Do you smoke a pipe?

Чи палите Ви люльку?
Chy palyte Vy lyul'ku?

75 [seventy-five]

giving reasons 1

75 [сімдесят п’ять]

75 [simdesyat p"yat’]

Щось обґрунтовувати 1

Shchos’ obgruntovuvaty 1

Why aren’t you coming?	Чому ви не приходите? Chomu vy ne prykhodyte?
The weather is so bad.	Погода дуже погана. Pohoda duzhe pohana.
I am not coming because the weather is so bad.	Я не прийду, тому що погода погана. YA ne pryÿdu, tomu shcho pohoda pohana.
Why isn’t he coming?	Чому він не приходить? Chomu vin ne prykhodyt’?
He isn’t invited.	Він не запрошений. Vin ne zaproshenyÿ.
He isn’t coming because he isn’t invited.	Він не прийде, тому що він не запрошений. Vin ne pryÿde, tomu shcho vin ne zaproshenyÿ.
Why aren’t you coming?	Чому ти не приходиш? Chomu ty ne prykhodysh?
I have no time.	Я не маю часу. YA ne mayu chasu.
I am not coming because I have no time.	Я не прийду, тому що я не маю часу. YA ne pryÿdu, tomu shcho ya ne mayu chasu.

75 [seventy-five]

giving reasons 1

75 [сімдесят п'ять]
75 [simdesyat p"yat']

Щось обґрунтовувати 1
Shchos' obgruntovuvaty 1

Why don't you stay?
Чому ти не залишаєшся?
Chomu ty ne zalyshayeshsya?

I still have to work.
Я повинен / повинна ще працювати.
YA povynen / povynna shche pratsyuvaty.

I am not staying because I still have to work.
Я не залишаюся, тому що я повинен / повинна ще працювати.
YA ne zalyshayusya, tomu shcho ya povynen / povynna shche pratsyuvaty.

Why are you going already?
Чому ви вже йдете?
Chomu vy vzhe ўdete?

I am tired.
Я втомлений / втомлена.
YA vtomlenyў / vtomlena.

I'm going because I'm tired.
Я йду, тому що я втомлений / втомлена.
YA ўdu, tomu shcho ya vtomlenyў / vtomlena.

Why are you going already?
Чому ви вже їдете?
Chomu vy vzhe ïdete?

It is already late.
Вже пізно.
Vzhe pizno.

I'm going because it is already late.
Я їду, тому що вже пізно.
YA ïdu, tomu shcho vzhe pizno.

76 [seventy-six]

giving reasons 2

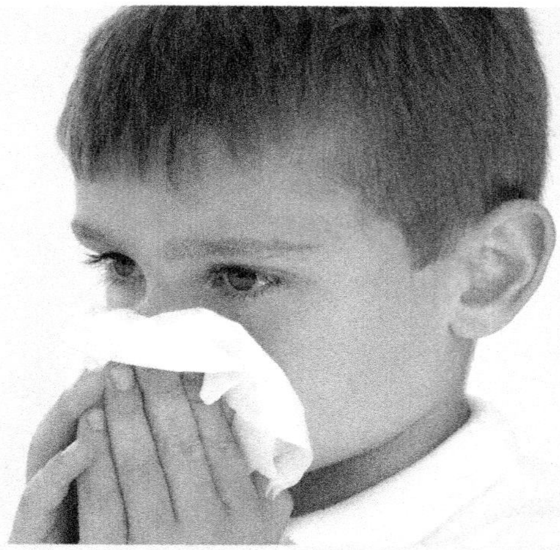

76 [сімдесят шість]
76 [simdesyat shist’]

Щось обґрунтовувати 2

Shchos’ obgruntovuvaty 2

Why didn’t you come? — Чому ти не прийшов / прийшла?
Chomu ty ne pryŷshov / pryŷshla?

I was ill. — Я був хворий. / Я була хвора.
YA buv khvoryŷ. / YA bula khvora.

I didn’t come because I was ill. — Я не прийшов / прийшла, тому що я був хворий / була хвора.
YA ne pryŷshov / pryŷshla, tomu shcho ya buv khvoryŷ / bula khvora.

Why didn’t she come? — Чому вона не прийшла?
Chomu vona ne pryŷshla?

She was tired. — Вона була втомлена.
Vona bula vtomlena.

She didn’t come because she was tired. — Вона не прийшла, тому що вона була втомлена.
Vona ne pryŷshla, tomu shcho vona bula vtomlena.

Why didn’t he come? — Чому він не прийшов?
Chomu vin ne pryŷshov?

He wasn’t interested. — Він не мав бажання.
Vin ne mav bazhannya.

He didn’t come because he wasn’t interested. — Він не прийшов, тому що він не мав бажання.
Vin ne pryŷshov, tomu shcho vin ne mav bazhannya.

76 [seventy-six]

giving reasons 2

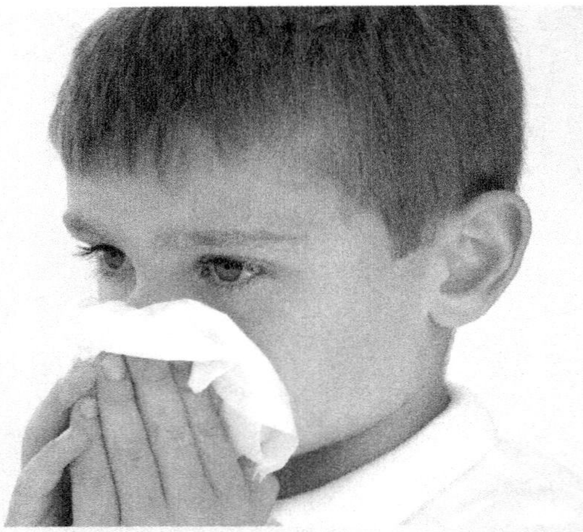

76 [сімдесят шість]
76 [simdesyat shist’]

Щось обґрунтовувати 2

Shchos’ obgruntovuvaty 2

Why didn’t you come?	Чому ви не прийшли? Chomu vy ne pryўshly?
Our car is damaged.	Наш автомобіль зламався. Nash avtomobil’ zlamavsya.
We didn’t come because our car is damaged.	Ми не прийшли, тому що наш автомобіль зламався. My ne pryўshly, tomu shcho nash avtomobil’ zlamavsya.
Why didn’t the people come?	Чому люди не прийшли? Chomu lyudy ne pryўshly?
They missed the train.	Вони не встигли на поїзд. Vony ne vstyhly na poïzd.
They didn’t come because they missed the train.	Вони не прийшли, тому що вони не встигли на поїзд. Vony ne pryўshly, tomu shcho vony ne vstyhly na poïzd.
Why didn’t you come?	Чому ти не прийшов / прийшла? Chomu ty ne pryўshov / pryўshla?
I was not allowed to.	Я не міг / могла. YA ne mih / mohla.
I didn’t come because I was not allowed to.	Я не прийшов / прийшла, тому що я не міг / могла. YA ne pryўshov / pryўshla, tomu shcho ya ne mih / mohla.

77 [seventy-seven]

giving reasons 3

77 [сімдесят сім]
77 [simdesyat sim]

Щось обґрунтовувати 3

Shchos' obgruntovuvaty 3

Why aren't you eating the cake?	Чому Ви не їсте торта? Chomu Vy ne ïste torta?
I must lose weight.	Я мушу схуднути. YA mushu skhudnuty.
I'm not eating it because I must lose weight.	Я його не їм, тому що я мушу схуднути. YA ÿoho ne ïm, tomu shcho ya mushu skhudnuty.
Why aren't you drinking the beer?	Чому Ви не п'єте пива? Chomu Vy ne p"yete pyva?
I have to drive.	Я повинен / повинна ще їхати. YA povynen / povynna shche ïkhaty.
I'm not drinking it because I have to drive.	Я його не п'ю, тому що я повинен / повинна ще їхати. YA ÿoho ne p'yu, tomu shcho ya povynen / povynna shche ïkhaty.
Why aren't you drinking the coffee?	Чому ти не п'єш кави? Chomu ty ne p"yesh kavy?
It is cold.	Вона холодна. Vona kholodna.
I'm not drinking it because it is cold.	Я її не п'ю, тому що вона холодна. YA ïï ne p'yu, tomu shcho vona kholodna.

77 [seventy-seven]

giving reasons 3

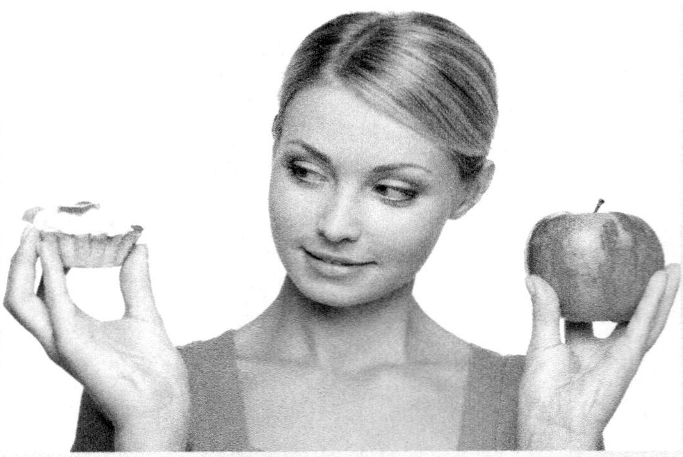

77 [сімдесят сім]
77 [simdesyat sim]

Щось обґрунтовувати 3
Shchos' obgruntovuvaty 3

Why aren't you drinking the tea?	Чому ти не п'єш чаю? Chomu ty ne p"yesh chayu?
I have no sugar.	Я не маю цукру. YA ne mayu tsukru.
I'm not drinking it because I don't have any sugar.	Я його не п'ю, тому що я не маю цукру. YA ÿoho ne p'yu, tomu shcho ya ne mayu tsukru.
Why aren't you eating the soup?	Чому Ви не їсте суп? Chomu Vy ne ïste sup?
I didn't order it.	Я його не замовляв / замовляла. YA ÿoho ne zamovlyav / zamovlyala.
I'm not eating it because I didn't order it.	Я його не їм, тому що я його не замовляв / замовляла. YA ÿoho ne ïm, tomu shcho ya ÿoho ne zamovlyav / zamovlyala.
Why don't you eat the meat?	Чому Ви не їсте м'яса? Chomu Vy ne ïste m"yasa?
I am a vegetarian.	Я вегетаріанець. YA vehetarianets'.
I'm not eating it because I am a vegetarian.	Я не їм це, тому що я вегетаріанець. YA ne ïm tse, tomu shcho ya vehetarianets'.

78 [seventy-eight]

Adjectives 1

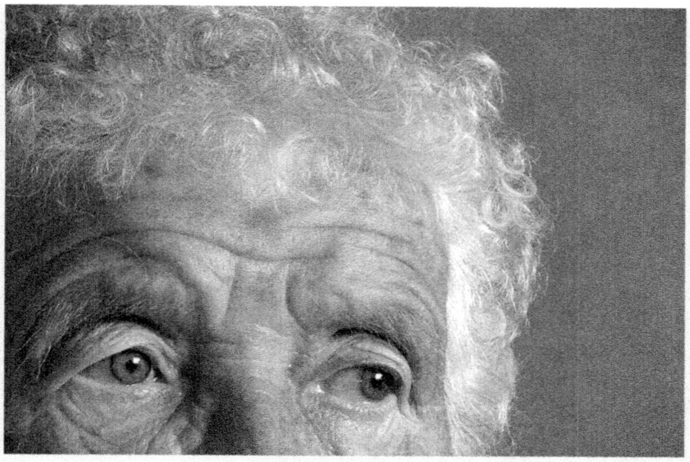

78 [сімдесят вісім]
78 [simdesyat visim]

Прикметники 1
Prykmetnyky 1

an old lady

стара жінка
stara zhinka

a fat lady

товста жінка
tovsta zhinka

a curious lady

допитлива жінка
dopytlyva zhinka

a new car

новий автомобіль
novyў avtomobil’

a fast car

швидкий автомобіль
shvydkyў avtomobil’

a comfortable car

зручний автомобіль
zruchnyў avtomobil’

a blue dress

синє плаття
synye plattya

a red dress

червоне плаття
chervone plattya

a green dress

зелене плаття
zelene plattya

78 [seventy-eight]

78 [сімдесят вісім]
78 [simdesyat visim]

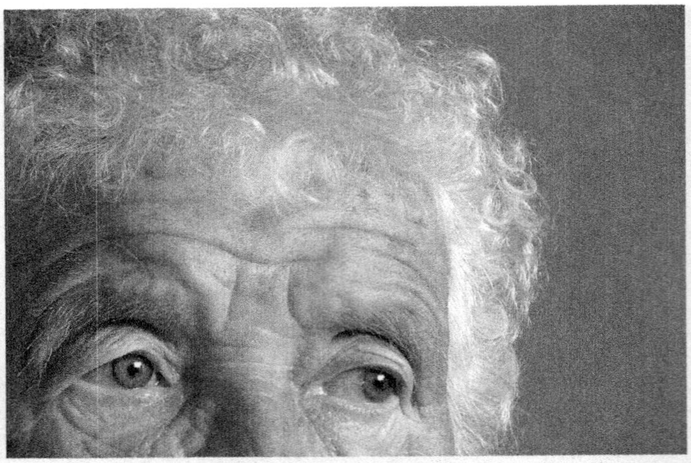

Adjectives 1

Прикметники 1
Prykmetnyky 1

a black bag	чорна сумка chorna sumka
a brown bag	коричнева сумка korychneva sumka
a white bag	біла сумка bila sumka
nice people	люб’язні люди lyub"yazni lyudy
polite people	ввічливі люди vvichlyvi lyudy
interesting people	цікаві люди tsikavi lyudy
loving children	милі діти myli dity
cheeky children	зухвалі діти zukhvali dity
well behaved children	слухняні діти slukhnyani dity

79 [seventy-nine]

79 [сімдесят дев’ять]
79 [simdesyat dev”yat’]

Adjectives 2

Прикметники 2
Prykmetnyky 2

I am wearing a blue dress.
На мені синє плаття.
Na meni synye plattya.

I am wearing a red dress.
На мені червоне плаття.
Na meni chervone plattya.

I am wearing a green dress.
На мені зелене плаття.
Na meni zelene plattya.

I’m buying a black bag.
Я купую чорну сумку.
YA kupuyu chornu sumku.

I’m buying a brown bag.
Я купую коричневу сумку.
YA kupuyu korychnevu sumku.

I’m buying a white bag.
Я купую білу сумку.
YA kupuyu bilu sumku.

I need a new car.
Мені потрібен новий автомобіль.
Meni potriben novyў avtomobil’.

I need a fast car.
Мені потрібен швидкий автомобіль.
Meni potriben shvydkyў avtomobil’.

I need a comfortable car.
Мені потрібен зручний автомобіль.
Meni potriben zruchnyў avtomobil’.

79 [seventy-nine]

79 [сімдесят дев’ять]
79 [simdesyat dev"yat']

Adjectives 2

Прикметники 2
Prykmetnyky 2

An old lady lives at the top.	Там нагорі живе стара жінка. Tam nahori zhyve stara zhinka.
A fat lady lives at the top.	Там нагорі живе товста жінка. Tam nahori zhyve tovsta zhinka.
A curious lady lives below.	Там внизу живе допитлива жінка. Tam vnyzu zhyve dopytlyva zhinka.
Our guests were nice people.	Наші гості були люб’язними людьми. Nashi hosti buly lyub'yaznymy lyud’my.
Our guests were polite people.	Наші гості були ввічливими людьми. Nashi hosti buly vvichlyvymy lyud’my.
Our guests were interesting people.	Наші гості були цікавими людьми. Nashi hosti buly tsikavymy lyud’my.
I have lovely children.	Я маю милих дітей. YA mayu mylykh diteў.
But the neighbours have naughty children.	Але сусіди мають зухвалих дітей. Ale susidy mayut’ zukhvalykh diteў.
Are your children well behaved?	Ваші діти чемні? Vashi dity chemni?

80 [eighty]

80 [вісімдесят]

80 [visimdesyat]

Adjectives 3

Прикметники 3

Prykmetnyky 3

She has a dog.	Вона має собаку. Vona maye sobaku.
The dog is big.	Собака великий. Sobaka velykyў.
She has a big dog.	Вона має великого собаку. Vona maye velykoho sobaku.
She has a house.	Вона має будинок. Vona maye budynok.
The house is small.	Будинок маленький. Budynok malen'kyў.
She has a small house.	Вона має маленький будинок. Vona maye malen'kyў budynok.
He is staying in a hotel.	Він живе в готелі. Vin zhyve v hoteli.
The hotel is cheap.	Готель дешевий. Hotel' deshevyў.
He is staying in a cheap hotel.	Він живе у дешевому готелі. Vin zhyve u deshevomu hoteli.

80 [eighty]

Adjectives 3

80 [вісімдесят]
80 [visimdesyat]

Прикметники 3
Prykmetnyky 3

He has a car.
Він має автомобіль.
Vin maye avtomobilʹ.

The car is expensive.
Автомобіль дорогий.
Avtomobilʹ dorohyy̆.

He has an expensive car.
Він має дорогий автомобіль.
Vin maye dorohyy̆ avtomobilʹ.

He reads a novel.
Він читає роман.
Vin chytaye roman.

The novel is boring.
Роман нудний.
Roman nudnyy̆.

He is reading a boring novel.
Він читає нудний роман.
Vin chytaye nudnyy̆ roman.

She is watching a movie.
Вона дивиться фільм.
Vona dyvytʹsya filʹm.

The movie is exciting.
Фільм захоплюючий.
Filʹm zakhoplyuyuchyy̆.

She is watching an exciting movie.
Вона дивиться захоплюючий фільм.
Vona dyvytʹsya zakhoplyuyuchyy̆ filʹm.

81 [eighty-one]

Past tense 1

81 [вісімдесят один]
81 [visimdesyat odyn]

Минулий час 1
Mynulyў chas 1

to write	Писати Pysaty
He wrote a letter.	Він писав листа. Vin pysav lysta.
And she wrote a card.	А вона написала листівку. A vona napysala lystivku.
to read	Читати Chytaty
He read a magazine.	Він читав журнал. Vin chytav zhurnal.
And she read a book.	А вона читала книгу. A vona chytala knyhu.
to take	Брати Braty
He took a cigarette.	Він узяв сигарету. Vin uzyav syharetu.
She took a piece of chocolate.	Вона взяла частину шоколадки. Vona vzyala chastynu shokoladky.

81 [eighty-one]

Past tense 1

81 [вісімдесят один]
81 [visimdesyat odyn]

Минулий час 1
Mynulyў chas 1

He was disloyal, but she was loyal.
Він був невірний, а вона була вірна.
Vin buv nevirnyў, a vona bula virna.

He was lazy, but she was hard-working.
Він був ледачий, а вона була старанна.
Vin buv ledachyў, a vona bula staranna.

He was poor, but she was rich.
Він був бідний, а вона була багата.
Vin buv bidnyў, a vona bula bahata.

He had no money, only debts.
Він не мав грошей, лише борги.
Vin ne mav hrosheў, lyshe borhy.

He had no luck, only bad luck.
Він не мав щастя, лише нещастя.
Vin ne mav shchastya, lyshe neshchastya.

He had no success, only failure.
Він не мав успіху, лише невдачі.
Vin ne mav uspikhu, lyshe nevdachi.

He was not satisfied, but dissatisfied.
Він не був задоволеним, а незадоволеним.
Vin ne buv zadovolenym, a nezadovolenym.

He was not happy, but sad.
Він не був щасливим, а нещасливим.
Vin ne buv shchaslyvym, a neshchaslyvym.

He was not friendly, but unfriendly.
Він не був приємним, а неприємним.
Vin ne buv pryyemnym, a nepryyemnym.

82 [eighty-two]

82 [вісімдесят два]
82 [visimdesyat dva]

Past tense 2

Минулий час 2
Mynulyŷ chas 2

Did you have to call an ambulance?
Ти мусив викликати машину швидкої допомоги?
Ty musyv vyklykaty mashynu shvydkoï dopomohy?

Did you have to call the doctor?
Ти мусив викликати лікаря?
Ty musyv vyklykaty likarya?

Did you have to call the police?
Ти мусив викликати поліцію?
Ty musyv vyklykaty politsiyu?

Do you have the telephone number? I had it just now.
Чи маєте Ви номер телефону? Я щойно його мав / мала.
Chy mayete Vy nomer telefonu? YA shchoŷno ŷoho mav / mala.

Do you have the address? I had it just now.
Чи маєте Ви адресу? Я щойно її мав / мала.
Chy mayete Vy adresu? YA shchoŷno ïï mav / mala.

Do you have the city map? I had it just now.
Чи маєте Ви мапу міста? Я щойно її мав / мала.
Chy mayete Vy mapu mista? YA shchoŷno ïï mav / mala.

Did he come on time? He could not come on time.
Чи прийшов він вчасно? Він міг затриматись.
Chy pryŷshov vin vchasno? Vin mih zatrymatys'.

Did he find the way? He could not find the way.
Чи знайшов він дорогу? Він не знайшов дорогу.
Chy znaŷshov vin dorohu? Vin ne znaŷshov dorohu.

Did he understand you? He could not understand me.
Чи зрозумів він тебе? Він не зрозумів мене.
Chy zrozumiv vin tebe? Vin ne zrozumiv mene.

82 [eighty-two]

Past tense 2

82 [вісімдесят два]
82 [visimdesyat dva]

Минулий час 2
Mynulyy̆ chas 2

Why could you not come on time?	Чому ти запізнився? Chomu ty zapiznyvsya?
Why could you not find the way?	Чому ти не знайшов дорогу? Chomu ty ne znay̆shov dorohu?
Why could you not understand him?	Чому ти не зрозумів його? Chomu ty ne zrozumiv y̆oho?
I could not come on time because there were no buses.	Я не міг / могла прийти вчасно, тому що не їздив жодний автобус. YA ne mih / mohla pryy̆ty vchasno, tomu shcho ne ïzdyv zhodnyy̆ avtobus.
I could not find the way because I had no city map.	Я не міг / могла знайти дорогу, тому що я не мав / мала мапи міста. YA ne mih / mohla znay̆ty dorohu, tomu shcho ya ne mav / mala mapy mista.
I could not understand him because the music was so loud.	Я не міг / могла його зрозуміти, тому що музика була занадто гучна. YA ne mih / mohla y̆oho zrozumity, tomu shcho muzyka bula zanadto huchna.
I had to take a taxi.	Я повинен був / повинна була узяти таксі. YA povynen buv / povynna bula uzyaty taksi.
I had to buy a city map.	Я повинен був / повинна була купити мапу міста. YA povynen buv / povynna bula kupyty mapu mista.
I had to switch off the radio.	Я повинен був / повинна була вимкнути радіо. YA povynen buv / povynna bula vymknuty radio.

83 [eighty-three]

Past tense 3

83 [вісімдесят три]
83 [visimdesyat try]

Минулий час 3
Mynulyў chas 3

to make a call

Телефонувати
Telefonuvaty

I made a call.

Я телефонував / телефонувала.
YA telefonuvav / telefonuvala.

I was talking on the phone all the time.

Я весь час телефонував / телефонувала.
YA ves' chas telefonuvav / telefonuvala.

to ask

Запитувати
Zapytuvaty

I asked.

Я запитав / запитала.
YA zapytav / zapytala.

I always asked.

Я запитував / запитувала завжди.
YA zapytuvav / zapytuvala zavzhdy.

to narrate

Розповідати
Rozpovidaty

I narrated.

Я розповів / розповіла.
YA rozpoviv / rozpovila.

I narrated the whole story.

Я розповів / розповіла цілу історію.
YA rozpoviv / rozpovila tsilu istoriyu.

83 [eighty-three]

Past tense 3

83 [вісімдесят три]
83 [visimdesyat try]

Минулий час 3
Mynulyў chas 3

to study	Вчитися Vchytysya
I studied.	Я вчився / вчилася. YA vchyvsya / vchylasya.
I studied the whole evening.	Я вчився / вчилася цілий вечір. YA vchyvsya / vchylasya tsilyў vechir.
to work	Працювати Pratsyuvaty
I worked.	Я працював / працювала. YA pratsyuvav / pratsyuvala.
I worked all day long.	Я працював / працювала весь день. YA pratsyuvav / pratsyuvala ves' den'.
to eat	Їсти Ïsty
I ate.	Я з'їв / з'їла. YA z"ïv / z"ïla.
I ate all the food.	Я з'їв / з'їла усю їжу. YA z"ïv / z"ïla usyu ïzhu.

84 [eighty-four]

84 [вісімдесят чотири]
84 [visimdesyat chotyry]

Past tense 4

Минулий час 4
Mynulyў chas 4

to read	Читати Chytaty
I read.	Я прочитав / прочитала. YA prochytav / prochytala.
I read the whole novel.	Я прочитав / прочитала цілий роман. YA prochytav / prochytala tsilyў roman.
to understand	Розуміти Rozumity
I understood.	Я зрозумів / зрозуміла. YA zrozumiv / zrozumila.
I understood the whole text.	Я зрозумів / зрозуміла цілий текст. YA zrozumiv / zrozumila tsilyў tekst.
to answer	Відповідати Vidpovidaty
I answered.	Я відповів / відповіла. YA vidpoviv / vidpovila.
I answered all the questions.	Я відповів / відповіла на всі питання. YA vidpoviv / vidpovila na vsi pytannya.

84 [eighty-four]

Past tense 4

84 [вісімдесят чотири]
84 [visimdesyat chotyry]

Минулий час 4
Mynulyў chas 4

I know that – I knew that.

Я це знаю – я це знав / я це знала.
YA tse znayu – ya tse znav / ya tse znala.

I write that – I wrote that.

Я пишу це – я написав це / я написала це.
YA pyshu tse – ya napysav tse / ya napysala tse.

I hear that – I heard that.

Я це чую – я це чув / я це чула.
YA tse chuyu – ya tse chuv / ya tse chula.

I'll get it – I got it.

Я принесу це – я приніс це / я принесла це.
YA prynesu tse – ya prynis tse / ya prynesla tse.

I'll bring that – I brought that.

Я принесу це – я приніс це / я принесла це.
YA prynesu tse – ya prynis tse / ya prynesla tse.

I'll buy that – I bought that.

Я куплю це – я купив це / я купила це.
YA kuplyu tse – ya kupyv tse / ya kupyla tse.

I expect that – I expected that.

Я чекаю цього – я чекав цього / я чекала цього.
YA chekayu ts'oho – ya chekav ts'oho / ya chekala ts'oho.

I'll explain that – I explained that.

Я поясню це – я пояснив це / я пояснила це.
YA poyasnyu tse – ya poyasnyv tse / ya poyasnyla tse.

I know that – I knew that.

Я знаю це – я знав це / я знала це.
YA znayu tse – ya znav tse / ya znala tse.

85 [eighty-five]

Questions – Past tense 1

85 [вісімдесят п’ять]

85 [visimdesyat p”yat’]

Питання – минулий час 1

Pytannya – mynulyў chas 1

How much did you drink?	Скільки Ви випили? Skil’ky Vy vypyly?
How much did you work?	Скільки Ви працювали? Skil’ky Vy pratsyuvaly?
How much did you write?	Скільки Ви написали? Skil’ky Vy napysaly?
How did you sleep?	Як Ви спали? Yak Vy spaly?
How did you pass the exam?	Як Ви здали іспит? Yak Vy zdaly ispyt?
How did you find the way?	Як Ви знайшли дорогу? Yak Vy znaўshly dorohu?
Who did you speak to?	З ким Ви говорили? Z kym Vy hovoryly?
With whom did you make an appointment?	З ким Ви домовилися? Z kym Vy domovylysya?
With whom did you celebrate your birthday?	З ким Ви святкували день народження? Z kym Vy svyatkuvaly den’ narodzhennya?

85 [eighty-five]

Questions – Past tense 1

85 [вісімдесят п’ять]

85 [visimdesyat p”yat’]

Питання – минулий час 1

Pytannya – mynulyў chas 1

Where were you? | Де Ви були?
De Vy buly?

Where did you live? | Де Ви жили?
De Vy zhyly?

Where did you work? | Де Ви працювали?
De Vy pratsyuvaly?

What did you suggest? | Що Ви рекомендували?
Shcho Vy rekomenduvaly?

What did you eat? | Що Ви їли?
Shcho Vy ïly?

What did you come to know? | Що Ви дізналися?
Shcho Vy diznalysya?

How fast did you drive? | Як швидко Ви їхали?
Yak shvydko Vy ïkhaly?

How long did you fly? | Як довго Ви летіли?
Yak dovho Vy letily?

How high did you jump? | Як високо Ви стрибнули?
Yak vysoko Vy strybnuly?

86 [eighty-six]

Questions – Past tense 2

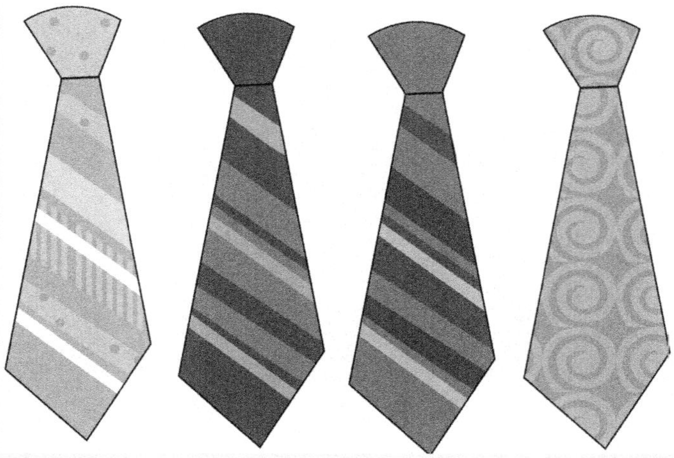

86 [вісімдесят шість]

86 [visimdesyat shist']

Питання – минулий час 2

Pytannya – mynulyў chas 2

Which tie did you wear?	Яку краватку ти носив? Yaku kravatku ty nosyv?
Which car did you buy?	Який автомобіль ти купив? Yakyў avtomobil' ty kupyv?
Which newspaper did you subscribe to?	Яку газету ти передплатив? Yaku hazetu ty peredplatyv?
Who did you see?	Кого ви бачили? Koho vy bachyly?
Who did you meet?	Кого Ви зустріли? Koho Vy zustrily?
Who did you recognize?	Кого Ви пізнали? Koho Vy piznaly?
When did you get up?	Коли Ви встали? Koly Vy vstaly?
When did you start?	Коли Ви почали? Koly Vy pochaly?
When did you finish?	Коли Ви припинили? Koly Vy prypynyly?

86 [eighty-six]

Questions – Past tense 2

86 [вісімдесят шість]
86 [visimdesyat shist′]

Питання – минулий час 2

Pytannya – mynulyў chas 2

Why did you wake up?	Чому Ви прокинулися? Chomu Vy prokynulysya?
Why did you become a teacher?	Чому Ви стали вчителем? Chomu Vy staly vchytelem?
Why did you take a taxi?	Чому Ви взяли таксі? Chomu Vy vzyaly taksi?
Where did you come from?	Звідки Ви прийшли? Zvidky Vy pryўshly?
Where did you go?	Куди Ви ходили? Kudy Vy khodyly?
Where were you?	Де Ви були? De Vy buly?
Who did you help?	Кому ти допоміг / допомогла? Komu ty dopomih / dopomohla?
Who did you write to?	Кому ти написав / написала? Komu ty napysav / napysala?
Who did you reply to?	Кому ти відповів / відповіла? Komu ty vidpoviv / vidpovila?

87 [eighty-seven]

87 [вісімдесят сім]
87 [visimdesyat sim]

Past tense of modal verbs 1

Модальні дієслова у минулому 1

Modal'ni diyeslova u mynulomu 1

We had to water the flowers.	Ми повинні були полити квіти. My povynni buly polyty kvity.
We had to clean the apartment.	Ми повинні були прибрати житло. My povynni buly prybraty zhytlo.
We had to wash the dishes.	Ми повинні були вимити посуд. My povynni buly vymyty posud.
Did you have to pay the bill?	Чи повинні ви були оплатити рахунок? Chy povynni vy buly oplatyty rakhunok?
Did you have to pay an entrance fee?	Чи повинні ви були заплатити за вхід? Chy povynni vy buly zaplatyty za vkhid?
Did you have to pay a fine?	Чи повинні ви були сплатити штраф? Chy povynni vy buly splatyty shtraf?
Who had to say goodbye?	Хто повинен був попрощатися? Khto povynen buv poproshchatysya?
Who had to go home early?	Хто повинен був йти рано додому? Khto povynen buv ўty rano dodomu?
Who had to take the train?	Хто повинен був їхати поїздом? Khto povynen buv ïkhaty poïzdom?

87 [eighty-seven]

87 [вісімдесят сім]
87 [visimdesyat sim]

Past tense of modal verbs 1

Модальні дієслова у минулому 1
Modal'ni diyeslova u mynulomu 1

We did not want to stay long.	Ми не хотіли залишитися надовго. My ne khotily zalyshytysya nadovho.
We did not want to drink anything.	Ми не хотіли нічого пити. My ne khotily nichoho pyty.
We did not want to disturb you.	Ми не хотіли заважати. My ne khotily zavazhaty.
I just wanted to make a call.	Я хотів / хотіла тільки що зателефонувати. YA khotiv / khotila til'ky shcho zatelefonuvaty.
I just wanted to call a taxi.	Я хотів / хотіла замовити таксі. YA khotiv / khotila zamovyty taksi.
Actually I wanted to drive home.	Я хотів / хотіла їхати додому. YA khotiv / khotila ïkhaty dodomu.
I thought you wanted to call your wife.	Я думав / думала, що ти хотів зателефонувати своїй дружині. YA dumav / dumala, shcho ty khotiv zatelefonuvaty svoïy druzhyni.
I thought you wanted to call information.	Я думав / думала, що ти хотів зателефонувати у довідкове бюро. YA dumav / dumala, shcho ty khotiv zatelefonuvaty u dovidkove byuro.
I thought you wanted to order a pizza.	Я думав / думала, що ти хотів замовити піцу. YA dumav / dumala, shcho ty khotiv zamovyty pitsu.

88 [eighty-eight]

Past tense of modal verbs 2

88 [вісімдесят вісім]
88 [visimdesyat visim]

Модальні дієслова у минулому 2
Modal’ni diyeslova u mynulomu 2

My son did not want to play with the doll.	Мій син не хотів бавитися лялькою. Miŷ syn ne khotiv bavytysya lyal’koyu.
My daughter did not want to play football / soccer (am.).	Моя дочка не хотіла грати у футбол. Moya dochka ne khotila hraty u futbol.
My wife did not want to play chess with me.	Моя жінка не хотіла грати в шахи зі мною. Moya zhinka ne khotila hraty v shakhy zi mnoyu.
My children did not want to go for a walk.	Мої діти не хотіли гуляти. Moï dity ne khotily hulyaty.
They did not want to tidy the room.	Вони не хотіли прибрати кімнату. Vony ne khotily prybraty kimnatu.
They did not want to go to bed.	Вони не хотіли йти спати. Vony ne khotily ŷty spaty.
He was not allowed to eat ice cream.	Йому не можна було їсти морозива. Ŷomu ne mozhna bulo ïsty morozyva.
He was not allowed to eat chocolate.	Йому не можна було їсти шоколад. Ŷomu ne mozhna bulo ïsty shokolad.
He was not allowed to eat sweets.	Йому не можна було їсти цукерок. Ŷomu ne mozhna bulo ïsty tsukerok.

88 [eighty-eight]

Past tense of modal verbs 2

88 [вісімдесят вісім]
88 [visimdesyat visim]

Модальні дієслова у минулому 2
Modal'ni diyeslova u mynulomu 2

I was allowed to make a wish.	Я міг / могла щось забажати. YA mih / mohla shchos' zabazhaty.
I was allowed to buy myself a dress.	Я міг / могла купити собі одяг. YA mih / mohla kupyty sobi odyah.
I was allowed to take a chocolate.	Я міг / могла узяти собі цукерку. YA mih / mohla uzyaty sobi tsukerku.
Were you allowed to smoke in the airplane?	Тобі можна було курити в літаку? Tobi mozhna bulo kuryty v litaku?
Were you allowed to drink beer in the hospital?	Тобі можна було пити в лікарні пиво? Tobi mozhna bulo pyty v likarni pyvo?
Were you allowed to take the dog into the hotel?	Тобі можна було взяти собаку в готель? Tobi mozhna bulo vzyaty sobaku v hotel'?
During the holidays the children were allowed to remain outside late.	На канікулах діти могли довго залишатися надворі. Na kanikulakh dity mohly dovho zalyshatysya nadvori.
They were allowed to play in the yard for a long time.	Вони могли довго грати у дворі. Vony mohly dovho hraty u dvori.
They were allowed to stay up late.	Вони могли довго не спати. Vony mohly dovho ne spaty.

89 [eighty-nine]

Imperative 1

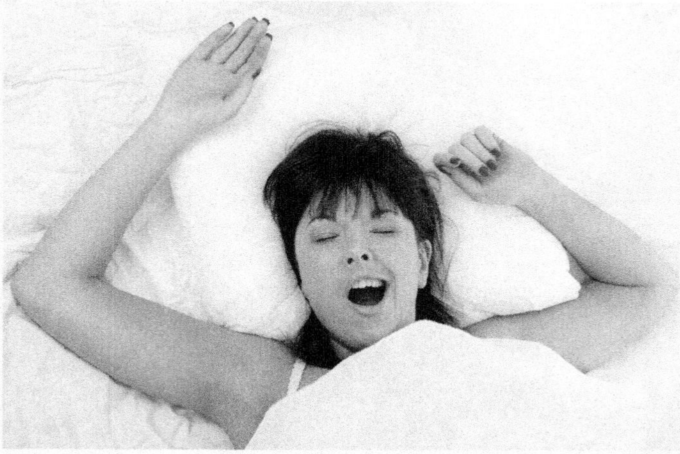

89 [вісімдесят дев’ять]
89 [visimdesyat dev”yat’]

Наказовий спосіб 1

Nakazovyў sposib 1

You are so lazy – don’t be so lazy!	Ти такий лінивий – не будь таким лінивим! Ty takyў linyvyў – ne bud’ takym linyvym!
You sleep for so long – don’t sleep so late!	Ти так довго спиш – не спи так довго! Ty tak dovho spysh – ne spy tak dovho!
You come home so late – don’t come home so late!	Ти приходиш так пізно – не приходь так пізно! Ty prykhodysh tak pizno – ne prykhod’ tak pizno!
You laugh so loudly – don’t laugh so loudly!	Ти смієшся так голосно – не смійся так голосно! Ty smiyeshsya tak holosno – ne smiўsya tak holosno!
You speak so softly – don’t speak so softly!	Ти говориш так тихо – не говори так тихо! Ty hovorysh tak tykho – ne hovory tak tykho!
You drink too much – don’t drink so much!	Ти п’єш дуже багато – не пий так багато! Ty p'yesh duzhe bahato – ne pyў tak bahato!
You smoke too much – don’t smoke so much!	Ти куриш дуже багато – не кури так багато! Ty kurysh duzhe bahato – ne kury tak bahato!
You work too much – don’t work so much!	Ти працюєш дуже багато – не працюй так багато! Ty pratsyuyesh duzhe bahato – ne pratsyuў tak bahato!
You drive too fast – don’t drive so fast!	Ти їдеш так швидко – не їдь так швидко! Ty ïdesh tak shvydko – ne ïd’ tak shvydko!

89 [eighty-nine]

Imperative 1

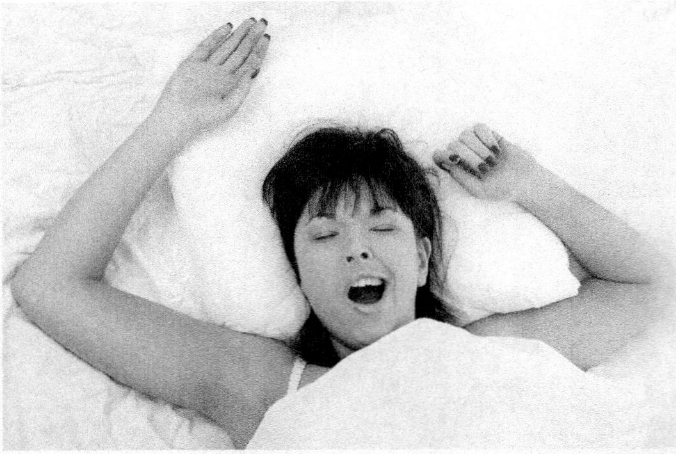

89 [вісімдесят дев’ять]
89 [visimdesyat dev"yat']

Наказовий спосіб 1
Nakazovyў sposib 1

Get up, Mr. Miller! — Встаньте, пане Мюллер!
Vstan’te, pane Myuller!

Sit down, Mr. Miller! — Сідайте, пане Мюллер!
Sidaўte, pane Myuller!

Remain seated, Mr. Miller! — Сидіть, пане Мюллер!
Sydit’, pane Myuller!

Be patient! — Майте терпіння!
Maўte terpinnya!

Take your time! — Не поспішайте!
Ne pospishaўte!

Wait a moment! — Зачекайте хвилинку!
Zachekaўte khvylynku!

Be careful! — Будьте обережні!
Bud’te oberezhni!

Be punctual! — Будьте пунктуальні!
Bud’te punktual’ni!

Don’t be stupid! — Не будьте безглузді!
Ne bud’te bez•hluzdi!

90 [ninety]

Imperative 2

90 [дев’яносто]
90 [dev”yanosto]

Наказовий спосіб 2
Nakazovyў sposib 2

Shave! | Поголися!
Poholysya!

Wash yourself! | Помийся!
Pomyўsya!

Comb your hair! | Причешися!
Prycheshysya!

Call! | Зателефонуй! Зателефонуйте!
Zatelefonuў! Zatelefonuўte!

Begin! | Починай! Починайте!
Pochynaў! Pochynaўte!

Stop! | Припини! Припиніть!
Prypyny! Prypynit’!

Leave it! | Облиш це! Облиште це!
Oblysh tse! Oblyshte tse!

Say it! | Скажи це! Скажіть це!
Skazhy tse! Skazhit’ tse!

Buy it! | Купи це! Купіть це!
Kupy tse! Kupit’ tse!

90 [ninety]

Imperative 2

90 [дев’яносто]
90 [dev"yanosto]

Наказовий спосіб 2

Nakazovyў sposib 2

Never be dishonest!	Ніколи не будь нечесним! Nikoly ne bud’ nechesnym!
Never be naughty!	Ніколи не будь зухвалим! Nikoly ne bud’ zukhvalym!
Never be impolite!	Ніколи не будь неввічливим! Nikoly ne bud’ nevvichlyvym!
Always be honest!	Завжди будь чесним! Zavzhdy bud’ chesnym!
Always be nice!	Завжди будь люб’язним! Zavzhdy bud’ lyub"yaznym!
Always be polite!	Завжди будь ввічливим! Zavzhdy bud’ vvichlyvym!
Hope you arrive home safely!	Щасливої дороги! Shchaslyvoï dorohy!
Take care of yourself!	Вважайте добре на себе! Vvazhaўte dobre na sebe!
Do visit us again soon!	Приходьте до нас скоро знову! Prykhod’te do nas skoro znovu!

91 [ninety-one]

91 [дев’яносто один]
91 [dev”yanosto odyn]

Subordinate clauses: that 1

Складнопідрядні речення із що 1
Skladnopidryadni rechennya iz shcho 1

Perhaps the weather will get better tomorrow.	Погода буде можливо кращою завтра. Pohoda bude mozhlyvo krashchoyu zavtra.
How do you know that?	Звідки Ви це знаєте? Zvidky Vy tse znayete?
I hope that it gets better.	Я сподіваюся, що вона буде кращою. YA spodivayusya, shcho vona bude krashchoyu.
He will definitely come.	Він напевно прийде. Vin napevno pryÿde.
Are you sure?	Це певне? Tse pevne?
I know that he’ll come.	Я знаю, що він прийде. YA znayu, shcho vin pryÿde.
He’ll definitely call.	Він напевно зателефонує. Vin napevno zatelefonuye.
Really?	Дійсно? Diÿsno?
I believe that he’ll call.	Я вірю, що він зателефонує. YA viryu, shcho vin zatelefonuye.

91 [ninety-one]

Subordinate clauses: that 1

91 [дев’яносто один]

91 [dev”yanosto odyn]

Складнопідрядні речення із що 1

Skladnopidryadni rechennya iz shcho 1

The wine is definitely old.	Вино напевно старе. Vyno napevno stare.
Do you know that for sure?	Чи знаєте Ви це напевне? Chy znayete Vy tse napevne?
I think that it is old.	Я припускаю, що воно старе. YA prypuskayu, shcho vono stare.
Our boss is good-looking.	Наш шеф добре виглядає. Nash shef dobre vyhlyadaye.
Do you think so?	Ви вважаєте? Vy vvazhayete?
I find him very handsome.	Я вважаю, що він виглядає навіть дуже добре. YA vvazhayu, shcho vin vyhlyadaye navit’ duzhe dobre.
The boss definitely has a girlfriend.	Шеф напевно має подругу. Shef napevno maye podruhu.
Do you really think so?	Ви дійсно так вважаєте? Vy diÿsno tak vvazhayete?
It is very possible that he has a girlfriend.	Цілком можливо, що він має подругу. Tsilkom mozhlyvo, shcho vin maye podruhu.

92 [ninety-two]

92 [дев’яносто два]
92 [dev”yanosto dva]

Subordinate clauses: that 2

Складнопідрядні речення із що 2
Skladnopidryadni rechennya iz shcho 2

I’m angry that you snore.
Мене дратує, що ти хропиш.
Mene dratuye, shcho ty khropysh.

I’m angry that you drink so much beer.
Мене дратує, що ти п’єш забагато пива.
Mene dratuye , shcho ty p'yesh zabahato pyva.

I’m angry that you come so late.
Мене дратує, що ти приходиш так пізно.
Mene dratuye, shcho ty prykhodysh tak pizno.

I think he needs a doctor.
Я думаю, що йому потрібен лікар.
YA dumayu, shcho ўomu potriben likar.

I think he is ill.
Я думаю, що він хворий.
YA dumayu, shcho vin khvoryў.

I think he is sleeping now.
Я думаю, що він тепер спить.
YA dumayu, shcho vin teper spyt’.

We hope that he marries our daughter.
Ми сподіваємося, що він одружиться з нашою дочкою.
My spodivayemosya, shcho vin odruzhyt’sya z nashoyu dochkoyu.

We hope that he has a lot of money.
Ми сподіваємося, що він має багато грошей.
My spodivayemosya, shcho vin maye bahato hrosheў.

We hope that he is a millionaire.
Ми сподіваємося, що він є мільйонером.
My spodivayemosya, shcho vin ye mil’ўonerom.

92 [ninety-two]

Subordinate clauses: that 2

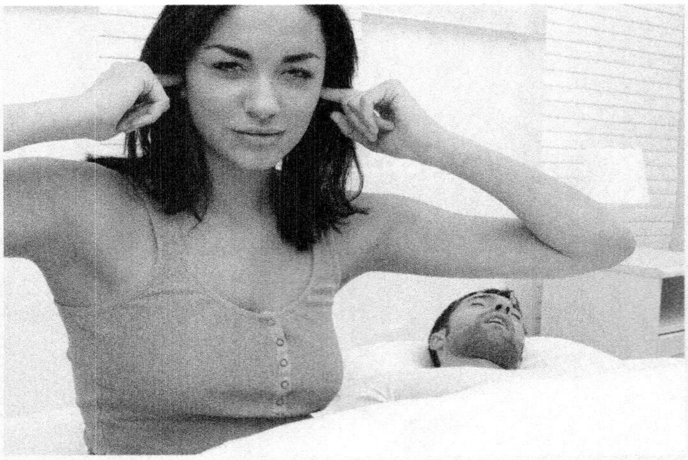

92 [дев’яносто два]
92 [dev”yanosto dva]

Складнопідрядні речення із що 2
Skladnopidryadni rechennya iz shcho 2

I heard that your wife had an accident.	Я чув / чула, що твоя дружина попала в аварію. YA chuv / chula, shcho tvoya druzhyna popala v avariyu.
I heard that she is in the hospital.	Я чув / чула, що вона лежить в лікарні. YA chuv / chula, shcho vona lezhyt’ v likarni.
I heard that your car is completely wrecked.	Я чув / чула, що твій автомобіль повністю розбитий. YA chuv / chula, shcho tviy̆ avtomobil’ povnistyu rozbytyy̆.
I’m happy that you came.	Мене тішить, що Ви прийшли. Mene tishyt’, shcho Vy pryy̆shly.
I’m happy that you are interested.	Мене тішить, що Вас це цікавить. Mene tishyt’, shcho Vas tse tsikavyt’.
I’m happy that you want to buy the house.	Мене тішить, що Ви хочете купити будинок. Mene tishyt’, shcho Vy khochete kupyty budynok.
I’m afraid the last bus has already gone.	Я припускаю, що останній автобус вже поїхав. YA prypuskayu, shcho ostanniy̆ avtobus vzhe poïkhav.
I’m afraid we will have to take a taxi.	Я припускаю, що ми повинні взяти таксі. YA prypuskayu, shcho my povynni vzyaty taksi.
I’m afraid I have no more money.	Я боюся, що я не маю при собі грошей. YA boyusya, shcho ya ne mayu pry sobi hroshey̆.

93 [ninety-three]

Subordinate clauses: if

93 [дев'яносто три]

93 [dev"yanosto try]

Складнопідрядні речення з чи

Skladnopidryadni rechennya z chy

I don't know if he loves me.
Я не знаю, чи він мене кохає.
YA ne znayu, chy vin mene kokhaye.

I don't know if he'll come back.
Я не знаю, чи він повернеться.
YA ne znayu, chy vin povernet'sya.

I don't know if he'll call me.
Я не знаю, чи він мені зателефонує.
YA ne znayu, chy vin meni zatelefonuye.

Maybe he doesn't love me?
Чи він мене любить?
Chy vin mene lyubyt'?

Maybe he won't come back?
Чи він повернеться?
Chy vin povernet'sya?

Maybe he won't call me?
Чи зателефонує він мені?
Chy zatelefonuye vin meni?

I wonder if he thinks about me.
Я запитую себе, чи думає він про мене.
YA zapytuyu sebe, chy dumaye vin pro mene.

I wonder if he has someone else.
Я запитую себе, чи має він іншу.
YA zapytuyu sebe, chy maye vin inshu.

I wonder if he lies.
Я запитую себе, чи він бреше.
YA zapytuyu sebe, chy vin breshe.

93 [ninety-three]

Subordinate clauses: if

93 [дев’яносто три]
93 [dev”yanosto try]

Складнопідрядні речення з чи
Skladnopidryadni rechennya z chy

Maybe he thinks of me?	Чи думає він про мене? Chy dumaye vin pro mene?
Maybe he has someone else?	Чи має він іншу? Chy maye vin inshu?
Maybe he tells me the truth?	Чи говорить він правду? Chy hovoryt’ vin pravdu?
I doubt whether he really likes me.	Я сумніваюся, що я дійсно йому подобаюсь. YA sumnivayusya, shcho ya diӯsno ӯomu podobayus’.
I doubt whether he’ll write to me.	Я сумніваюся, що він мені напише. YA sumnivayusya, shcho vin meni napyshe.
I doubt whether he’ll marry me.	Я сумніваюся, що він зі мною одружиться. YA sumnivayusya, shcho vin zi mnoyu odruzhyt’sya.
Does he really like me?	Чи дійсно я йому подобаюсь? Chy diӯsno ya ӯomu podobayus’?
Will he write to me?	Чи дійсно він мені напише? Chy diӯsno vin meni napyshe?
Will he marry me?	Чи дійсно він зі мною одружиться? Chy diӯsno vin zi mnoyu odruzhyt’sya?

94 [ninety-four]

Conjunctions 1

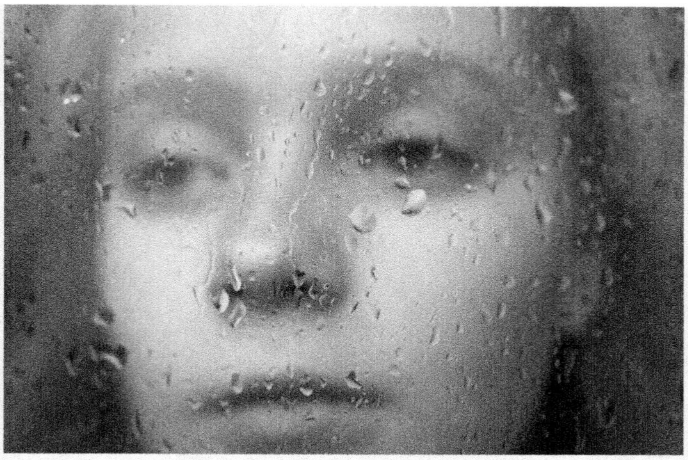

94 [дев'яносто чотири]
94 [dev"yanosto chotyry]

Сполучники 1
Spoluchnyky 1

Wait until the rain stops.
Зачекай доки перестане йти дощ.
Zachekaў doky perestane ўty doshch.

Wait until I'm finished.
Зачекай доки я буду готовий / готова.
Zachekaў doky ya budu hotovyў / hotova.

Wait until he comes back.
Зачекай доки він повернеться.
Zachekaў doky vin povernet'sya.

I'll wait until my hair is dry.
Я чекаю доки моє волосся висохне.
YA chekayu doky moye volossya vysokhne.

I'll wait until the film is over.
Я чекаю до кінця фільму.
YA chekayu do kintsya fil'mu.

I'll wait until the traffic light is green.
Я чекаю на зелене світло.
YA chekayu na zelene svitlo.

When do you go on holiday?
Коли ти їдеш у відпустку?
Koly ty ïdesh u vidpustku?

Before the summer holidays?
Ще перед літніми канікулами?
Shche pered litnimy kanikulamy?

Yes, before the summer holidays begin.
Так, ще до того, як почнуться літні канікули.
Tak, shche do toho, yak pochnut'sya litni kanikuly.

94 [ninety-four]

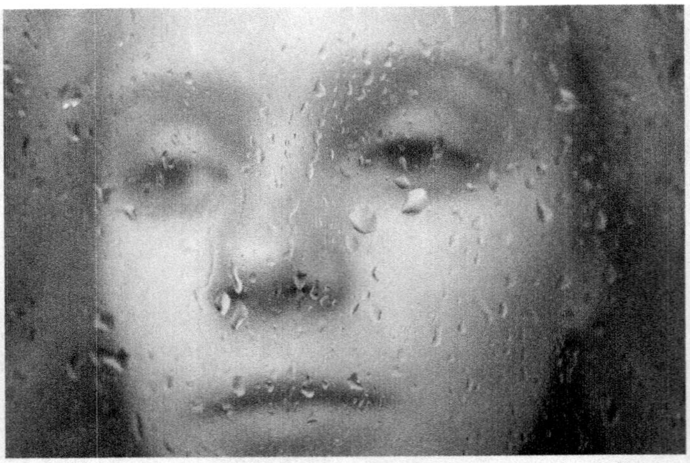

94 [дев’яносто чотири]
94 [dev”yanosto chotyry]

Conjunctions 1

Сполучники 1
Spoluchnyky 1

Repair the roof before the winter begins.	Полагоди дах, перш ніж зима почнеться. Polahody dakh, persh nizh zyma pochnet’sya.
Wash your hands before you sit at the table.	Помий руки, перш ніж ти сідатимеш за стіл. Pomyў ruky, persh nizh ty sidatymesh za stil.
Close the window before you go out.	Закрий вікно, перш ніж підеш геть. Zakryў vikno, persh nizh pidesh het’.
When will you come home?	Коли ти прийдеш додому? Koly ty pryўdesh dodomu?
After class?	Після заняття? Pislya zanyattya?
Yes, after the class is over.	Так, після заняття. Tak, pislya zanyattya.
After he had an accident, he could not work anymore.	Після аварії він не міг більше працювати. Pislya avariï vin ne mih bil’she pratsyuvaty.
After he had lost his job, he went to America.	Після того як він втратив роботу, він поїхав до Америки. Pislya toho yak vin vtratyv robotu, vin poïkhav do Ameryky.
After he went to America, he became rich.	Після того як він переїхав до Америки, він став багатим. Pislya toho yak vin pereïkhav do Ameryky, vin stav bahatym.

95 [ninety-five]

95 [дев’яносто п’ять]
95 [dev”yanosto p”yat’]

Conjunctions 2

Сполучники 2
Spoluchnyky 2

Since when is she no longer working?
Відколи вона більше не працює?
Vidkoly vona bil’she ne pratsyuye?

Since her marriage?
Від одруження?
Vid odruzhennya?

Yes, she is no longer working since she got married.
Так, вона більше не працює з того часу, як вона одружилася.
Tak, vona bil’she ne pratsyuye z toho chasu, yak vona odruzhylasya.

Since she got married, she’s no longer working.
З того часу, як вона одружилася, вона більше не працює.
Z toho chasu, yak vona odruzhylasya, vona bil’she ne pratsyuye.

Since they have met each other, they are happy.
Відтоді, як вони знаються, вони щасливі.
Vidtodi, yak vony znayut’sya, vony shchaslyvi.

Since they have had children, they rarely go out.
З того часу як вони мають дітей, вони виходять рідко.
Z toho chasu yak vony mayut’ diteў, vony vykhodyat’ ridko.

When does she call?
Коли вона телефонує?
Koly vona telefonuye?

When driving?
Під час їзди?
Pid chas ïzdy?

Yes, when she is driving.
Так, тоді коли вона керує авто.
Tak, todi koly vona keruye avto.

95 [ninety-five]

95 [дев'яносто п'ять]
95 [dev"yanosto p"yat']

Conjunctions 2

Сполучники 2
Spoluchnyky 2

She calls while she drives.	Вона телефонує тоді, коли вона керує авто. Vona telefonuye todi, koly vona keruye avto.
She watches TV while she irons.	Вона дивиться телевізор тоді, коли вона прасує. Vona dyvyt'sya televizor todi, koly vona prasuye.
She listens to music while she does her work.	Вона слухає музику тоді, коли вона робить свої справи. Vona slukhaye muzyku todi, koly vona robyt' svoï spravy.
I can't see anything when I don't have glasses.	Я нічого не бачу, якщо я без окулярів. YA nichoho ne bachu, yakshcho ya bez okulyariv.
I can't understand anything when the music is so loud.	Я нічого не розумію, якщо музика така голосна. YA nichoho ne rozumiyu, yakshcho muzyka taka holosna.
I can't smell anything when I have a cold.	Я нічого не відчуваю, якщо я маю нежить. YA nichoho ne vidchuvayu, yakshcho ya mayu nezhyt'.
We'll take a taxi if it rains.	Ми беремо таксі, якщо йде дощ. My beremo taksi, yakshcho ўde doshch.
We'll travel around the world if we win the lottery.	Ми будемо подорожувати навколо світу, якщо ми виграємо в лотерею. My budemo podorozhuvaty navkolo svitu, yakshcho my vyhrayemo v lotereyu.
We'll start eating if he doesn't come soon.	Ми почнемо їсти, якщо він зараз не прийде. My pochnemo ïsty, yakshcho vin zaraz ne pryўde.

96 [ninety-six]

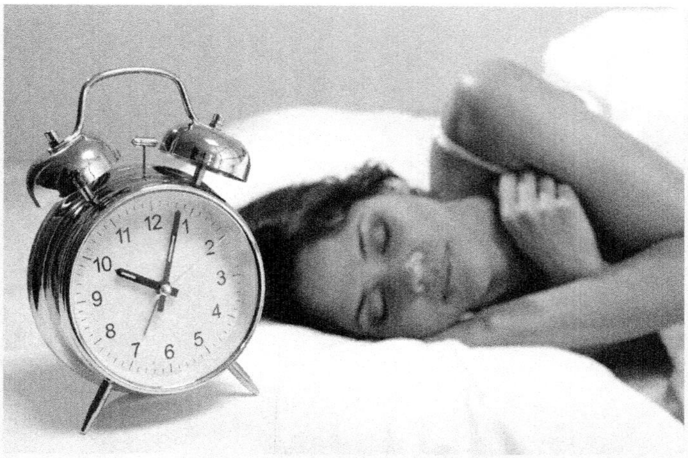

96 [дев’яносто шість]

96 [dev”yanosto shist’]

Conjunctions 3

Сполучники 3

Spoluchnyky 3

I get up as soon as the alarm rings.	Я встану, як тільки задзвонить будильник. YA vstanu, yak til’ky zadzvonyt’ budyl’nyk.
I become tired as soon as I have to study.	Я стаю втомлений / втомлена, як тільки мені потрібно вчитися. YA stayu vtomlenyў / vtomlena, yak til’ky meni potribno vchytysya.
I will stop working as soon as I am 60.	Я перестану працювати, як тільки мені виповниться 60 років. YA perestanu pratsyuvaty, yak til’ky meni vypovnyt’sya 60 rokiv.
When will you call?	Коли Ви зателефонуєте? Koly Vy zatelefonuyete?
As soon as I have a moment.	Як тільки я матиму час. Yak til’ky ya matymu chas.
He’ll call, as soon as he has a little time.	Він зателефонує, як тільки він матиме трохи часу. Vin zatelefonuye, yak til’ky vin matyme trokhy chasu.
How long will you work?	Як довго ви будете працювати? Yak dovho vy budete pratsyuvaty?
I’ll work as long as I can.	Я буду працювати, доки я можу. YA budu pratsyuvaty, doky ya mozhu.
I’ll work as long as I am healthy.	Я буду працювати, доки я здоровий / здорова. YA budu pratsyuvaty, doky ya zdorovyў / zdorova.

96 [ninety-six]

96 [дев’яносто шість]
96 [dev”yanosto shist’]

Conjunctions 3

Сполучники 3
Spoluchnyky 3

He lies in bed instead of working.	Він лежить в ліжку, замість того щоб працювати. Vin lezhyt’ v lizhku, zamist’ toho shchob pratsyuvaty.
She reads the newspaper instead of cooking.	Вона читає газету, замість того щоб готувати їжу . Vona chytaye hazetu, zamist’ toho shchob hotuvaty ïzhu .
He is at the bar instead of going home.	Він сидить у пивній, замість того щоб іти додому. Vin sydyt’ u pyvniў, zamist’ toho shchob ity dodomu.
As far as I know, he lives here.	Наскільки я знаю, він живе тут. Naskil’ky ya znayu, vin zhyve tut.
As far as I know, his wife is ill.	Наскільки я знаю, його жінка хвора. Naskil’ky ya znayu, ўoho zhinka khvora.
As far as I know, he is unemployed.	Наскільки я знаю, він безробітний. Naskil’ky ya znayu, vin bezrobitnyў.
I overslept; otherwise I’d have been on time.	Я проспав / проспала, інакше я був би / була би вчасно. YA prospav / prospala, inakshe ya buv by / bula by vchasno.
I missed the bus; otherwise I’d have been on time.	Я пропустив / пропустила автобус, інакше я був би / була би вчасно. YA propustyv / propustyla avtobus, inakshe ya buv by / bula by vchasno.
I didn’t find the way / I got lost; otherwise I’d have been on time.	Я не знайшов / знайшла дороги, інакше я був би / була би вчасно. YA ne znaўshov / znaўshla dorohy, inakshe ya buv by / bula by vchasno.

97 [ninety-seven]

97 [дев’яносто сім]
97 [dev"yanosto sim]

Conjunctions 4

Сполучники 4
Spoluchnyky 4

He fell asleep although the TV was on.
Він заснув, хоча телевізор був ввімкнутий.
Vin zasnuv, khocha televizor buv vvimknutyў.

He stayed a while although it was late.
Він ще залишився, хоча було вже пізно.
Vin shche zalyshyvsya, khocha bulo vzhe pizno.

He didn’t come although we had made an appointment.
Він не прийшов, хоча ми домовились.
Vin ne pryўshov, khocha my domovylys'.

The TV was on. Nevertheless, he fell asleep.
Телевізор був ввімкнутий. А він все одно заснув.
Televizor buv vvimknutyў. A vin vse odno zasnuv.

It was already late. Nevertheless, he stayed a while.
Було Вже пізно. А він все одно ще залишився.
Bulo Vzhe pizno. A vin vse odno shche zalyshyvsya.

We had made an appointment. Nevertheless, he didn’t come.
Ми домовились. Не зважаючи на це, він не прийшов.
My domovylys'. Ne zvazhayuchy na tse, vin ne pryўshov.

Although he has no license, he drives the car.
Хоча він не має водійських прав, він їздить на машині.
Khocha vin ne maye vodiўs'kykh prav, vin ïzdyt' na mashyni.

Although the road is slippery, he drives so fast.
Хоча на вулиці ожеледиця, він їздить швидко.
Khocha na vulytsi ozheledytsya, vin ïzdyt' shvydko.

Although he is drunk, he rides his bicycle.
Хоча він п’яний, він їде на велосипеді.
Khocha vin p'yanyў, vin ïde na velosypedi.

97 [ninety-seven]

97 [дев’яносто сім]
97 [dev”yanosto sim]

Conjunctions 4

Сполучники 4
Spoluchnyky 4

Despite having no licence / license (am.), he drives the car.	Він не має водійських прав. Проте він їздить на машині. Vin ne maye vodiy̆s’kykh prav. Prote vin ïzdyt’ na mashyni.
Despite the road being slippery, he drives fast.	На вулиці ожеледиця. Проте він їздить швидко. Na vulytsi ozheledytsya. Prote vin ïzdyt’ shvydko.
Despite being drunk, he rides the bike.	Він п’яний. Проте він їде на велосипеді. Vin p”yanyy̆. Prote vin ïde na velosypedi.
Although she went to college, she can’t find a job.	Вона не може знайти роботи, хоча вона має освіту. Vona ne mozhe znay̆ty roboty, khocha vona maye osvitu.
Although she is in pain, she doesn’t go to the doctor.	Вона не йде до лікаря, хоча вона має болі. Vona ne y̆de do likarya, khocha vona maye boli.
Although she has no money, she buys a car.	Вона купує автомобіль, хоча вона не має грошей. Vona kupuye avtomobil’, khocha vona ne maye hroshey̆.
She went to college. Nevertheless, she can’t find a job.	Вона отримала освіту. Проте вона не може знайти роботу. Vona otrymala osvitu. Prote vona ne mozhe znay̆ty robotu.
She is in pain. Nevertheless, she doesn’t go to the doctor.	Вона має болі. Проте вона не йде до лікаря. Vona maye boli. Prote vona ne y̆de do likarya.
She has no money. Nevertheless, she buys a car.	Вона не має грошей. Проте купує автомобіль. Vona ne maye hroshey̆. Prote kupuye avtomobil’.

98 [ninety-eight]

Double connectors

98 [дев'яносто вісім]
98 [dev"yanosto visim]

Подвійні сполучники
Podviÿni spoluchnyky

The journey was beautiful, but too tiring.	Поїздка була гарна, але дуже напружена. Poïzdka bula harna, ale duzhe napruzhena.
The train was on time, but too full.	Потяг прибув вчасно, але був переповнений. Potyah prybuv vchasno, ale buv perepovnenyÿ.
The hotel was comfortable, but too expensive.	Готель був затишний, але надто дорогий. Hotel' buv zatyshnyÿ, ale nadto dorohyÿ.
He'll take either the bus or the train.	Він їде або автобусом, або потягом. Vin ïde abo avtobusom, abo potyahom.
He'll come either this evening or tomorrow morning.	Він прийде або сьогодні ввечері або завтра вранці. Vin pryÿde abo s'ohodni vvecheri abo zavtra vrantsi.
He's going to stay either with us or in the hotel.	Він зупиниться або у нас або в готелі. Vin zupynyt'sya abo u nas abo v hoteli.
She speaks Spanish as well as English.	Вона говорить і іспанською, і англійською . Vona hovoryt' i ispans'koyu, i anhliÿs'koyu .
She has lived in Madrid as well as in London.	Вона жила і в Мадриді і в Лондоні. Vona zhyla i v Madrydi i v Londoni.
She knows Spain as well as England.	Вона знає як Іспанію так і Англію. Vona znaye yak Ispaniyu tak i Anhliyu.

98 [ninety-eight]

98 [дев’яносто вісім]
98 [dev”yanosto visim]

Double connectors

Подвійні сполучники
Podviÿni spoluchnyky

He is not only stupid, but also lazy.	Він не тільки дурний, але й ледачий. Vin ne til'ky durnyÿ, ale ÿ ledachyÿ.
She is not only pretty, but also intelligent.	Вона не тільки вродлива, але й розумна. Vona ne til'ky vrodlyva, ale ÿ rozumna.
She speaks not only German, but also French.	Вона говорить не тільки німецькою, але й французькою. Vona hovoryt' ne til'ky nimets'koyu, ale ÿ frantsuz'koyu.
I can neither play the piano nor the guitar.	Я не граю ані на фортепіано, ані на гітарі. YA ne hrayu ani na fortepiano, ani na hitari.
I can neither waltz nor do the samba.	Я не вмію танцювати ані вальсу, ані самби. YA ne vmiyu tantsyuvaty ani val'su, ani samby.
I like neither opera nor ballet.	Мені не подобається ані опера, ані балет. Meni ne podobayet'sya ani opera, ani balet.
The faster you work, the earlier you will be finished.	Чим швидше ти працюєш, тим раніше закінчиш. Chym shvydshe ty pratsyuyesh, tym ranishe zakinchysh.
The earlier you come, the earlier you can go.	Чим раніше ти прийдеш, тим раніше зможеш піти. Chym ranishe ty pryÿdesh, tym ranishe zmozhesh pity.
The older one gets, the more complacent one gets.	Чим старшою стає людина, тим вона більше любить затишок. Chym starshoyu staye lyudyna, tym vona bil'she lyubyt' zatyshok.

99 [ninety-nine]

99 [дев’яносто дев’ять]
99 [dev”yanosto dev”yat’]

Genitive

Родовий відмінок
Rodovyў vidminok

my girlfriend’s cat — кішка моєї подруги
kishka moyeї podruhy

my boyfriend’s dog — собака мого друга
sobaka moho druha

my children’s toys — іграшки моїх дітей
ihrashky moїkh diteў

This is my colleague’s overcoat. — це – пальто мого колеги.
tse – pal’to moho kolehy.

That is my colleague’s car. — Це – автомобіль моєї колеги.
Tse – avtomobil’ moyeї kolehy.

That is my colleagues’ work. — Це – робота моїх колег.
Tse – robota moїkh koleh.

The button from the shirt is gone. — Ґудзик відлетів від сорочки.
Gudzyk vidletiv vid sorochky.

The garage key is gone. — Немає ключа від гаража.
Nemaye klyucha vid harazha.

The boss’ computer is not working. — Комп’ютер керівника зіпсований.
Komp'yuter kerivnyka zipsovanyў.

99 [ninety-nine]

99 [дев’яносто дев’ять]
99 [dev”yanosto dev”yat’]

Genitive

Родовий відмінок
Rodovyў vidminok

Who are the girl’s parents?	Хто батьки дівчинки? Khto bat’ky divchynky ?
How do I get to her parents’ house?	Як пройти до будинку її батьків? Yak proўty do budynku її bat’kiv?
The house is at the end of the road.	Будинок в кінці вулиці. Budynok v kintsi vulytsi.
What is the name of the capital city of Switzerland?	Як називається столиця Швейцарії? Yak nazyvayet’sya stolytsya Shveўtsariї?
What is the title of the book?	Як називається книга? Yak nazyvayet’sya knyha?
What are the names of the neighbour’s / neighbor’s (am.) children?	Як звати дітей сусідів? Yak zvaty diteў susidiv?
When are the children’s holidays?	Коли у дітей канікули? Koly u diteў kanikuly?
What are the doctor’s consultation times?	Коли приймає лікар? Koly pryўmaye likar?
What time is the museum open?	Коли музей відчинений? Koly muzeў vidchynenyў?

100 [one hundred]

100 [сто]
100 [sto]

Adverbs

Прислівники
Pryslivnyky

already – not yet	вже один раз – ще ніколи vzhe odyn raz – shche nikoly
Have you already been to Berlin?	Ви вже були в Берліні? Vy vzhe buly v Berlini?
No, not yet.	Ні, ще ніколи. Ni, shche nikoly.
someone – no one	Хто-небудь – ніхто Khto-nebud' – nikhto
Do you know someone here?	Ви знаєте тут кого-небудь? Vy znayete tut koho-nebud'?
No, I don't know anyone here.	Ні, я не знаю тут нікого. Ni, ya ne znayu tut nikoho.
a little longer – not much longer	ще – більше ні shche – bil'she ni
Will you stay here a little longer?	Ви тут ще надовго залишаєтеся? Vy tut shche nadovho zalyshayetesya?
No, I won't stay here much longer.	Ні, я залишаюся ненадовго. Ni, ya zalyshayusya nenadovho.

100 [one hundred]

100 [сто]
100 [sto]

Adverbs

Прислівники
Pryslivnyky

something else – nothing else
ще щось – більше нічого
shche shchos' – bil'she nichoho

Would you like to drink something else?
Хочете ще щось випити?
Khochete shche shchos' vypyty?

No, I don't want anything else.
Ні, я не хочу більше нічого.
Ni, ya ne khochu bil'she nichoho.

something already – nothing yet
вже щось – ще нічого
vzhe shchos' – shche nichoho

Have you already eaten something?
Ви вже щось з'їли?
Vy vzhe shchos' z"ïly?

No, I haven't eaten anything yet.
Ні, я ще нічого не їв / їла.
Ni, ya shche nichoho ne ïv / ïla.

someone else – no one else
ще хто-небудь – більше ніхто
shche khto-nebud' – bil'she nikhto

Does anyone else want a coffee?
Бажає ще хто-небудь кави?
Bazhaye shche khto-nebud' kavy?

No, no one else.
Ні, більше ніхто.
Ni, bil'she nikhto.

ЯCHI O4I

= Klare Augen Kampfeinheit die mit Drohnen Kämpfen

Die Drohnenkrieger der Ukraine (Arte)

Printed in Great Britain
by Amazon

42029402R00117